A Bridge Between East and West

At first sight, any normal exhibition of some of the more aggressive traditional Oriental fighting methods, such as k'ung fu or karate, may persuade the non-initiated that he or she is viewing just another form of hand-to-hand combat, similar to (if not quite the same as) normal Western boxing, wrestling, and the like.

Although it is perfectly true that a certain proficiency in the martial skills of the East can result from assiduous physical exercise and training, there are some regions of martial arts activity which patently transcend the normal, and border on the supernormal.

Moving with the Wind examines closely this supernatural nature of the Martial Arts—i.e., the "Magick of the Martial Arts," and includes several basic martial arts exercises related to the development of the mysterious force known in China as chi, and in Japan as ki.

This book is for all who seriously desire to improve their perception of themselves and of the universe. It offers some practical suggestions as a prelude to involvement in any of the martial arts—or as a taste of what the martial arts are all about. It also shows how the use of martial arts exercises can be a powerful part of any magickal practice

For the already practicing martial artist, this book explains the origins, philosophy, and techniques of his or her own system, as set against the origins, philosophy, and techniques of other systems.

About the Authors

Brian Crowley has made a lifelong study of Eastern, Middle Eastern and other metaphysical, philosophical, and religious systems, and is the author of several books on metaphysical and sporting topics. Esther Crowley, a noted psychic artist and former portrait sculptor, is a teacher and author of yoga and meditation topics, and co-author, with her husband, of two books and audio tapes, one on Oriental martial arts, and the other examining esoteric traditions and usage of sacred words of power. The Crowleys live in Australia, but travel extensively, lecturing and researching in their fields.

To Write to the Authors

If you wish to contact the authors or would like more information about this book, please write to the authors in care of Llewellyn Worldwide, and we will forward your request. Both the authors and publisher appreciate hearing from you and learning of your enjoyment of this book and how it has helped you. Llewellyn Worldwide cannot guarantee that every letter written to the authors can be answered, but all will be forwarded. Please write to:

Brian & Esther Crowley
c/o Llewellyn Worldwide
P.O. Box 64383-134, St. Paul, MN 55164-0383, U.S.A.

Please enclose a self-addressed, stamped envelope for reply, or $1.00 to cover costs. If outside U.S.A., enclose international postal reply coupon.

Free Catalog from Llewellyn

For more than ninety years Llewellyn has brought its readers knowledge in the fields of metaphysics and human potential. Learn about the newest books in spiritual guidance, natural healing, astrology, occult philosophy and more. Enjoy book reviews, new age articles, a calendar of events, plus current advertised products and services. To get your free copy of *Llewellyn's New Worlds*, send your name and address to:

Llewellyn's New Worlds
P.O. Box 64383-134, St. Paul, MN 55164-0383, U.S.A.

Moving with the Wind

Magick and healing in the martial arts

Brian Crowley
with
Esther Crowley

1994
Llewellyn Publications
St. Paul, Minnesota, 55164–0383, U.S.A.

FIRST EDITION, 1993
Second Printing, 1994

Cover design by Christopher Wells
Interior illustrations by Esther Crowley

Library of Congress Cataloging-in-Publication Data
Crowley, Brian, 1937–
    Moving with the wind : magick and healing in the martial arts / Brian & Esther Crowley.
        p.   cm. —
    ISBN 0-87542-134-2
        1. Martial arts—Philosophy. 2. Mysticism. I. Crowley, Esther, 1937–   . II. Title.
    GV1101.C764   1993   92-40420
    796.8—dc20 CIP

Llewellyn Publications
A Division of Llewellyn Worldwide, Ltd.
St. Paul, Minnesota 55164-0383, U.S.A.

Dedication

This book is respectfully dedicated to all those great masters and teachers of the martial arts who, down the centuries, have led their pupils' footsteps firmly and correctly onto that straight and glorious path which is known simply as "The Way."

What we call footprints were of course produced by feet,
but they are not actually the feet.
In the same way, books were written by sages,
but they are not the sages.

Ko Hung (284-364 C.E.)
Nei Ping

Acknowledgments

For special help in producing this book, we give thanks to our close friend Koji (Daido) Yada, former Shinto priest, for seven years a Buddhist monk, master of several Japanese healing arts, and an expert in the sword art known as Niten-Ichi-Ryu, and to martial arts instructor Tom Crone of Minneapolis, Minnesota, for his detailed criticism of the manuscript and for his many sage suggestions for its improvement. A note of gratitude is also due to Carl Llewellyn Weschcke for his encouragement and guiding hand throughout, especially in providing us with a fuller understanding of the Western Magickal Tradition.

Other Books by Brian Crowley
The Springbok and the Kangaroo
Concise Key to Numerology
Currie Cup Story
Calypso Cavaliers
Cricket's Exiles
A History of Australian Batting
A History of Australian Bowling
The Face on Mars (with J. J. Hurtak)
Australia's Greatest Cricket Characters
Australia's Tennis Greats
A Cavalcade of International Cricketers
The Great Aussie Sausage Book (with Erich Schaal)
The Zulu Bone Oracle
Return to Mars (with Anthony Pollock)
Cradle Days of Australian Cricket (with Pat Mullins)
Hotting Up
The Magic World of the Zulu
   (with Credo Vuzamazulu Mutwa) (forthcoming)

Books by Esther Crowley
The Living Waters of Yoga & Meditation
Joga in die Buitelug
Love is Life

Books by Brian and Esther Crowley
Understanding the Oriental Martial Arts
Japanese Gods of Luck (forthcoming)
Words of Power (Llewellyn Publications)

Contents

☯ Preface: The Way

What does martial arts practice really have to offer the West—other than a way to display extraordinary physical ability or to win in a fight?

Lao Tzu, founder of the philosophical system known as Tao (pronounced "Da-o" and meaning "The Way"), a system which has had a profound influence over the genesis and growth of the martial arts, points out in his classic *Tao te-Ching* that "A tree that is unbending is easily broken."

Anyone who is remotely associated with any of the many disciplines available to us for self-improvement, self-understanding, self-control, and healing will see in this statement not only advice relating to personal adaptability in circumstances of direct action, but also a suggestion that we might consider being even more flexible than we currently are in our use of available knowledge and/or techniques.

A certain proficiency in the martial skills of the East can result from assiduous physical exercise and training, but there are some regions which patently transcend the normal and border on the supernormal.

When one hears of an octogenarian just five feet tall and of very slight build simultaneously throwing six burly opponents across a room without moving from within a small chalk circle drawn upon the floor, there can be no doubt that something extraordinary is occurring; not to mention numerous instances on record of sundry martial artists being able to cut in half a pile of boards, bricks, or tiles with a bare hand, stop a raging bull with a single blow, or even claims that involve the simulation of invisibility, instantaneous bodily healing, prolongation of vigorous life into old age, and the use of sound to immobilize an opponent. All this would appear to be more like the work of a shaman than an athlete.

How does one contact and control the mysterious so-called ch'i energy which makes all of these feats possible? How can this energy be used in everyday life?

The Oriental martial arts, in a broad application, can be viewed as a "bridge" between Eastern and Western esoteric-type systems that are connected with personal holistic self-improvement—which includes special emphasis on the healing arts, also traditionally associated with martial arts activity.

This book is directed toward those people who seriously desire to improve their perception of themselves and of the universe—be they already practicing martial artists interested in a concise update on disciplines other than their own (and of some essential connections), or persons currently involved in some other physical, spiritual, magickal, and/or shamanistic practice, or simply searching for a suitable "pathway" in life.

Anyone (not already a martial artist) who, after reading this book, is inclined to go further along the road exemplified by the tree bending but not breaking in the wind, is expressly directed toward joining an accredited school of any particular chosen martial art. Selecting such a school (or teacher) is perhaps best accomplished by "shopping around," via research of the subject in accredited magazines, reading serious books on the subject and/or visiting several training studios prior to making a decision.

As a parting statement we would like to impress on our readers that, for anyone to appreciate the philosophical and/or spiritual aspects of the martial arts, it is not essential to actually partake in the physical training involved. The magick of the martial arts lies in the unity it prescribes. Ch'i or Universal energy remains ch'i energy, no matter what we may term it, and no matter what methods we may use to invoke it. The true Way of the Martial Arts is but one of many roads to the crest of the hill we call enlightenment. Beyond lies a timeless journey in a single eternal day.

1 ☯ Magick and the martial arts

The universe is process and the process is in me.
When I fight this process or ignore it, I am in trouble.
When I move with it, something happens . . .

Al Chung-liang Huang
Embrace Tiger, Return to Mountain

In the East, participation in the martial arts embraces all aspects of human activity, from spiritual through physical. This can raise the Oriental fighting arts into an area beyond that of mere hand-to-hand combat. A common feature is the striving for a state of total awareness, not achieved through any intellectual analysis, but intuitively. Certain magickal processes also appear to be at work which can defy rational explanation.

A clue as to where "magick"—as we recognize the term from the Western occult tradition—first enters the arena of the martial arts may be contained in the meaning applied to the word itself: i.e., "The use of various techniques, generally regarded as occult or 'hidden,' in order to penetrate the barriers imposed by the material plane so as to be able to connect with and operate within the spiritual realms which lie beyond that plane."

1

In order to distinguish between the merely illusory magic of the stage variety, and ceremonial and other types of magic that actually work with natural, but sometimes unseen forces of the universe, the term "magick" has come much into use in recent times. We will, accordingly, stick with this term. It is also of importance to note at the outset that we specifically exclude any reference in the present work to the sleight-of-hand and other techniques of the ordinary stage magician/entertainer, some of which have unfortunately been adapted from time to time for use by unscrupulous and/or outrightly fraudulent martial arts instructors. Sadly, many reports of supposedly phenomenal feats demonstrated by certain martial arts "gurus" are no more than trickery, or the result of the reporter's own enthusiasm and/or lack of discernment, but there still remain those exceptions which defy all rational explanation.

On magick

Magick has been with us since the first humans appeared on our planet, and probably originated in an early desire to wield power over natural forces. It has always been closely linked with religious and spiritual notions, the basic religious impulse being generally one of awe and worship of a god or gods in whom are vested supernatural powers. Science, on the other hand, tries to explain, in purely physical terms, how everything works. The practicing magician, however, endeavors to bend the laws of nature to his/her will, and is more interested in "what works" than with "why" or "how" things work.

Down the ages, two primary forms of magick have evolved: that performed in harmony with natural, cosmic laws and forces—generally referred to as "white magick"; and that which devolves around gratification of the individual magician's own desires and ambitions—i.e., "black magick." The former can usually only be accomplished by a person who develops a noble, self-disciplined, and dedicated attitude toward the art. In our present context, these mentioned qualities and attitudes can also be said to be essential prerequisites for the true martial artist. Without exception, the cornerstones of all martial arts systems are sincerity, discipline, and dedication, and some of the results of this training, as we have already observed, can quite easily be termed magickal. Also of importance to note is that martial arts techniques and training can be *seen* to work.

Normally, the practice of magick involves utilization of various physical paraphernalia, structured rituals, mental images, incantations etc., and/or meditation techniques. As another visible connection between magick and the martial arts, similar items and forms may also be seen in use among martial artists, each of the Eastern fighting disciplines having its own unique gear and/or garb, set of pre- and post-combat rituals, and special form of meditation-type techniques—as a complement to actual physical training.

The paradox

When any practitioner of *k'ung fu, karate, t'ai ch'i chuan, aikido, taekwon do* (or any of the other major fighting systems) squares up to an opponent, he/she participates in a ritual which reflects the integrated spiritual, philosophical, psychical, and practical efforts of millions of martial arts exponents over thousands of years. This emphasis is well in line with the renewed interest in the West in recent years in the more positive attributes of the warrior. These include the capacity to confront death with equanimity (which is also central to most Eastern religious teachings, such as Buddhism, for instance, as an important element in ultimate spirituality), to overcome the need for violent action through complete mastery of fighting techniques, and the development of true will power (which stems from the developed unconscious and not from a conscious "gritting of the teeth" attitude).

Chinese character denoting "ch'i"

In the East, the threefold spirit-mind-body participation lying at the heart of all martial arts activity is closely bound up with many ancient cosmological practices and beliefs: Buddhism, Taoism, and Shintoism; healing arts, such as acupuncture and *shiatsu*; those opposite but inseparable forces of nature known as yin and yang; and the related-to-all concept of ch'i—the mysterious universal force or power apparently available to all of us and especially those who are prepared to undergo the required disciplinary training. Special emphasis is also placed on an almost meditative state to be attained by the martial artist, particularly that of the "Zen variety." There is a subtle replacement of the power of the intellect with that of intuitive action. Zen, in fact, possesses no theory, being an "inner knowing" with no specified dogma involved. The power of the mind and/or spirit is considered infinite, while that of the physical body is limited. How this all works in relation to the importance of actual body movements will be touched on later.

Some might, indeed, be tempted to describe proficiency in the martial arts as: "The ability to perform physically impossible actions through occult development" (which also gives us another rather neat definition for any magickal practice, anywhere!).

A bridge between East and West

In the East, it has been almost universally the case for martial artists to favor the spiritual over the physical, but this is certainly not always as evident in the West—due possibly to the pressures exerted by a more materialistic society. It may also be said that in the East there is usually an adjustment made to the individual's life-style in order to meet the demands of any chosen martial arts school (and/or, for that matter, any spiritual/magickal discipline). In the West, the contrary is normally true; the relevant discipline is more often than not adjusted to fit in with the individual's already existing life-style (although prolonged practice of any martial art can, and usually does, result in some changes eventually being made to that life-style).

The fact is that the whole fabric of traditional social life in most Oriental countries is geared in many ways toward appreciation of certain hidden forces at play in any person's life, in the functioning of society, and in relation to the world and the cosmos itself. Therefore, it becomes correspondingly easier for anyone living in most Asian countries to center their lives around spiritual-type disciplines that recognize an extension of life beyond the physical. On the contrary, in the more materialistic West—where science has generally denied the existence of any occult forces at play in our lives—it is no simple matter to centralize one's activities around any specified martial arts teaching, or, for that matter, any magickal or spiritual practices that place premier emphasis on the non-physical life.

Because its practice has, in part at least, become almost universally accepted in the West, perhaps the greatest role to be played by the martial arts in the future will be to bridge this gap in attitudes—bringing East and West into closer, more harmonious union, for the benefit of all, materially and spiritually. In addition, as it grows in popularity, and if certain of its more mystical elements can be brought more to the fore, the martial arts may also help in a further opening up of western attitudes toward things esoteric. This may lead to a wider acceptance of other systems of self-discipline, self-development, and self-transcendence that are not based on the sometimes narrowly defined strictures contained in the "more acceptable" teachings of Christianity, Judaism, Islam, and other orthodox religions.

Moreover, those people involved in Western magickal systems (ceremonial, Wiccan, shamanistic, etc.), if they can be made more aware of the true essence of martial arts forms, might become more inclined to incorporate certain martial arts-type exercises in their own routines—simply because of their deep connection with age-old proven systems of mind-body discipline and energy control, that are, in any event, also part of the essential magickal traditions of the East.

Two distinct approaches

Although certain forms of specialized one-on-one combat have been practiced in the East for centuries, it is only during the past forty years or so that the martial arts secrets of the Orient have been made freely available to the West. Yet, in this short space of time, participation in k'ung fu, karate, judo, and the rest has become a noticeable part of the way of life of millions of people in the Western world. We have already noted that, in the Eastern context, martial arts exponents are not solely meant to become experts in the perpetration of physical violence. At their very foundations, the disciplines of most martial arts systems call for full use of all of the remarkable powers of the body, mind, and spirit of any individual for the purpose of overcoming an attack by an opponent, using a minimum of violence, and preferably through the use of no perceptible force at all—or, better still, to even avoid the conflict in the first instance. But in our present day world there appears to be a dichotomy of approach to practice of the martial arts. One way is based on violence and aggression under the guise of self-improvement; the other, in accord with the highest principles of the fighting arts, aims at eventual diminishment of violence as a preparation for the attainment of true self-understanding.

Where the fighting arts, as practiced in the East, still tend to differ from those now so popular in the West is in the subtle introduction into the Eastern systems of certain

moral, philosophical, and spiritual/magickal compo-
nents which raise them beyond mere methods of overcoming an attack in the purely physical sense. In the
West, if one is to judge primarily by the image projected
by many books and magazines, and most films, about the
various fighting systems, it would seem that the principal
emphasis has become almost totally associated with the
physical side of the combat arts, very frequently only as a
devastating maiming or killing process.

During our research for this present work, we came
across several instances where fairly well-known martial
arts personalities of the West have written books or articles in which they have actually disparaged the esoteric
side of their art. Some Western martial combat teachers
have, however, made a point of introducing spiritual elements into the training curriculum, but they appear to be
few and far between. It is possible that a seeming fascina-
tion in the West with the more aggressive aspects of the
Eastern fighting systems is just another visible extension
of the growing ethic of violence that so permeates almost
all of life in many of our modern cities. If, at this time,
there was to be a movement toward a more philosophi-
cal/spiritual attitude in the teaching of martial arts in the
West, apart from the obvious personal benefits to be
gained by current and potential martial artists, an important model of behavior might also be created for non-
martial artists to follow. As an ideal, the result might
eventually lead toward a swifter metamorphosis of our
growing culture of violence into a culture of mutual
respect and peace.

Healing

The important role played by healing in the history and development of the martial arts is frequently overlooked, or dismissed with perfunctory reference in training and in literature about the subject. Later, we will be enlarging upon this somewhat neglected side of the fighting arts, and will also offer several suggested healing methods and health-promoting exercises. When it comes to health and healing within the context of the Oriental philosophical and martial arts combat systems, special emphasis is always placed on the concept of ch'i energy. Because of its overriding importance in all martial arts activity, the subject of ch'i is dealt with separately.

For the present, the important fact to note is that behind each of the Oriental fighting systems there lies an indispensable collection of healing methods on many levels—physical, mental, and psychical. Moreover, some of the better-known Eastern therapeutic systems seem to have come either directly out of various martial arts teachings, or to have been profoundly influenced by the vast body of knowledge of the workings of the human bodily vehicle (or vehicles) put together by masters of those disciplines down through the centuries.

The strength within

Confucius, who is perhaps the most quoted in the West of all Chinese philosophers, once wrote: "What the superior man seeks is in himself. What the small man seeks is in others." In keeping with this profound statement from centuries ago, the paradox which lies at the center of all martial arts activity eventually leads the pupil to discover for him/herself that the greatest and most abundant strength is, indeed, to be found within, and not through concerted physical activity. What remains to be developed by any individual participant in any of the martial arts forms, once this discovery has been made, is controlled discrimination in the use of this inner strength, or power—defined by the Chinese as *ch'i*, and known to the Japanese as *ki*. This psychophysical energy is generally harnessed through directed action of the body and mind, in association with correct breathing. Special postures and movements are also important—the theory being that the recommended movements would, in any event, be those that would intuitively flow into being once the correct spiritual connection is made.

Participation in any martial arts discipline should bring with it not only enhancement of any individual's ability to defend him/herself, but the stirrings of a growing philosophical understanding. This should, ideally, lead to a deeper self-awareness, compassion for all fellow beings, attunement with nature itself, and the realization that the ultimate objective behind the fighting disciplines is to actually transcend the need for any form of violent action.

This process of personal alchemical transformation is perhaps the true, ultimate magick of the martial arts.

2 ☯ The art of energy conversion

Nothing in the world can be compared to water for its
weak and yielding nature; yet in attacking the hard
and the strong nothing proves better than it.
For there is no alternative to it.
The weak can overcome the strong and the yielding can
overcome the hard.
This all the world knows but does not practice.

Lao-tzu
Tao te-Ching

Followers of the long-running television drama series
"Kung Fu" may recall the dramatic sequence involving
principal actor David Carradine in which he was made to
overcome a series of deadly obstacles positioned in the
tunnel that took him out of the monastery, at which he
had received his training, to a new life in the world outside. The obstacle course was designed to test to the
utmost his k'ung fu skill, including, in particular, his
spontaneous intuitive responses. If he failed, he died; if
successful he had one more frightening hurdle to overcome, a test that would also serve to mark him with his
true identity for life. At the final gate barring exit from the

temple, the young aspirant would be compelled to lift in his bare arms a red-hot, metal urn emblazoned on each side with the Chinese dragon symbol. In the act of so doing, he would brand his arms forever with the twin-dragon insignia of the fighting priest of Shaolin—the master of k'ung fu.

This magickal, ceremonial testing of a person considered ready to leave the monastery of his training was, in reality, a known feature of the rigorous initiation undergone by young monks at the original Shaolin temple, considered to be the true spiritual home of the martial arts—although there has been a claim that the martial arts first evolved out of the calisthenic system called *Tao Yin* practiced by the legendary Yellow Emperor, Hwang Ti, who ruled China for a century during the third millennium B.C.E. and has been credited as the author of the famous *Nei Ching*, "The Yellow Emperor's Classic of Internal Medicine." It has, however, been ascertained by scholars that the *Nei Ching* is actually a synthesis of the writings of many Chinese doctors in the third or second century B.C.E. summarizing the practical knowledge of prior centuries, and there is no direct proof of any connection between Hwang Ti and the martial arts. Nor is there any documented proof of the verity of the old Chinese saying: "All the martial arts known under heaven began in Shaolin."

Notwithstanding its shadowy origins, the results of the Shaolin tradition can be seen in almost every city of the world, from Shanghai to San Francisco, and all the way back again to the Song Shan mountain monastery in northern China where the enigmatic sixth-century, India-born fighting monk Bodhidharma (known as Dharuma to the Japanese—legendary founder of the philosophical system now known as Zen Buddhism—first demonstrated his self-defense system known as "eighteen hands of the Lo-han" to his fellow monks. If credence is to be attached to the tale of Bodhidharma, the so-called martial arts may have experienced their genesis from within the

Bodhidharma—legendary founder of the Shaolin martial arts.

more gentle and spiritually oriented disciplines of yoga and Buddhist meditation.

War arts and ch'i-k'ung

It has been claimed that, under the active encouragement of the Chinese government, some 100 million people on mainland China take part in *wu shu* training at the present time—more than all the martial arts trainees found in the rest of the world combined. The expression wu shu means literally "war-arts," but has taken on the connotation of "national sport" in China. As a general definition "martial arts" means "fighting arts" and in its wider sense must be taken to include any form of formalized and studied fighting art, both Eastern and Western, such as, for instance, pistol shooting. However, for the purpose of our present study, the term is used to exclusively describe the traditional oriental forms of unarmed and armed combat performed by individual combatants.

The Chinese wu shu martial arts family today contains some 200 different styles of "hard" and "soft" school k'ung fu within its parameters—many of them dramatic and spectacular routines designed for visually thrilling entertainment. In reality, k'ung fu training techniques taught outside China represent but the tip of an enormous iceberg. Fantastic demonstrations by wu shu experts of the so-called art of *ch'i-k'ung* (or gigong) include the smashing with a large hammer of concrete blocks placed upon an exponent's chest, or the taking of a sword or spear blow, and emerging unscathed. Such experts are known as *ying-ch'i-k'ung* and, in the manner of the

Malaysian or South African Cape Malay "khalifa" performer, they are able to withstand the effects of swords, sharp spears, knives, and even meat cleavers without any piercing of the skin.

The technique employed by the ying-ch'i-k'ung involves the direction of vital ch'i energy to that part of the body which is to take the blow of the hammer or sword. This type of energy is also used in the breaking of objects, as has also been widely demonstrated in the West by karate experts. Using breathing and other exercises, a ch'i-k'ung adept can chop his way through a pile of bricks or tiles with a single blow from the side of his hand or even break free from a pair of steel handcuffs.

Touch of death

In the terminology of the practitioner of ch'i-k'ung, the ability to extend the power of ch'i to beyond the physical body is known as *nui-k'ung*—a word carrying the connotation "inner power"—a concept found deep within Taoist and Buddhist philosophical teachings. Some may wish to term it "magick."

In the oftimes paradoxical world of the martial artist, nui-k'ung can apparently also be used as a healing force, enabling masters of the art to heal injuries with the touch of a hand. Obversely, it is alleged that the nui-k'ung principle can be used to kill as well as to cure. Certain masters of k'ung fu are reputed to be able to administer the so-called "touch of death," or *dim muk*, to a vital spot on the body, at a prescribed time of the day, resulting in a delayed effect that will only manifest days, weeks, or even months after its application. The victim would feel no immediate discomfort and his/her subsequent illness and/or death at a later stage would come as a complete surprise.

The sudden and unexpected death, in 1973, of celebrated k'ung fu expert Bruce Lee not only brought to a close an era that had seen the transformation of the ancient art of Chinese temple boxing from an almost occult occupation into a modern fighting discipline (and an entertainment of universal appeal), but also fired rumors of assassination through use of the fabled "touch of death." However, an official inquest disclosed that the actual cause of the youthful k'ung fu screen hero's death was an edema of the brain caused by a painkilling drug, equagesic, to which he was reportedly allergic. True believers in the *dim muk* theory as related to Lee's passing will be quick to point out that the "touch of death" made it appear that their hero had died of natural causes. However, it might also be appropriate to note here that caution should perhaps be exercised in ascribing a "magickal" element back of all unexplained aspects of the martial arts and their associated techniques and offshoots.

In passing, it is valid to note that few individuals since the wise old Bodhidharma, himself, have influenced the martial arts movement as much as the charismatic Bruce Lee, whose name became a household word around the world, and who died, a legend in his own times, when still only in his twenties. Notwithstanding the possibility that some of his influence has been patently negative, by emphasizing the more brutish aspects of the martial arts, watching Bruce Lee in action was like observing the reincarnation of one of the legendary k'ung fu masters of the dim, distant past. His speed of movement was almost supernatural. He could send an opponent hurtling several feet from a blow that started an inch

Bruce Lee

away from the sparring partner's chest. His superbly coordinated floating punch from a range of between an inch and three inches was a dramatic feature of his uniquely fluid style. Always the experimenter, he developed his own system called *jeet kune-do*—"jeet" means to intercept, or to explode; "kune" means fist; "do" (tao) means the way. His fighting system has been described as the most fluid of the martial arts, direct and simple in its execution, and with all of its movements related directly to maximum efficiency.

What is not generally known is that the young jeet kune-do master's life was not all high leaps and kicks and stormy nunchaku battles with screen assassins. There was a serious side to his nature that only some of his closest colleagues and students were privileged to observe. In an interview with Erle Montaigue in *Australian Fighting Arts* (Vol. 11, No. 3), Dan Inosanto, a former pupil of Bruce Lee and a leading instructor in jeet kune-do, revealed that, although his teacher was known at times to make fun of meditation in training, ". . . the first thing on his own training schedule was meditation."

Inosanto noted that, although Lee pointed his students in one way—primarily toward the physical side of the martial arts—"he pointed himself in another way," the fact being that Bruce Lee himself practiced ch'i-k'ung, or chi power development, and was "heavily into esoteric studies." One of his favorite methods was the use of positive affirmations as a mind programming tool. He was apparently also very interested in acupuncture, the Chinese healing art involving the placement of thin, sharp needles in the body at special "meridian" points, in order to facilitate healing.

High kicks are a feature of some k'ung fu systems.

Style of the ultimate truth

When it comes to the well-known and now almost universal Japanese martial art known as karate (and with no intention of belittling the efforts of any other Japanese masters of the art, past and present), speak of the subject anywhere in the world today, and the name of Masutatsu Oyama will almost certainly come up somewhere in the conversation. Oyama's books on martial arts are probably more widely read than any others. His karate style, called *kyokushinkai* (literally "style of the ultimate truth"), is one of the most effective of all karate techniques. He is regarded by many as the greatest karate-ka of them all. He is also a notable "mystic" of the martial arts who has gained great success in translating ki force into practical power on the physical level.

Oyama was born in 1923 in Korea. At the age of nine he was already a wu shu practitioner and was influenced by Korean and Chinese forms of martial arts before he became a student of karate founder, Ginchin Funakoshi, at his Shotokan karate school in Tokyo, Japan. Built like an ox, and with the strength to match, Oyama could have passed as a sumo wrestler. He was also an incredible athlete, and a grim-faced personality in the ring who probably frightened the life out of as many opponents with his fierce and uncompromising look as those overcome by his superior karate skill.

Not particularly happy with the shotokan style of karate—which he considered too weak and too preoccupied with straight line movements—Oyama became, for a while, something of a recluse. He lived alone in meditation in the mountains for two and a half years while formulating his own unique karate style. To practice his highly individual striking technique, Oyama would go to the local slaughter-house and take on a bull bare-handed. On a number of occasions he felled and killed an animal with a single punch and, in one much-publicized battle, snapped off a four-inch diameter bull's horn at the root. He was also known to put on a demonstration in which he would outrun a bull, just to demonstrate that he was able to do so, should the necessity arise.

Meditation versus training

Oyama introduced to karate the wu shu art of ch'i-k'ung, breaking in half a stack of solid objects such as boards, bricks, and tiles with a single bare-handed chop (Oyama himself once smashed through 30 tiles with a single blow). His spectacular performances contributed much toward the later popularity of this form of martial arts display and his kyokushinkai was the first major karate style to incorporate block-breaking power blows—the Japanese art of *tamashiwara*. Kyokushinkai karate involves rugged training and tough conditioning. During the 1970s, Oyama introduced the concept of "knock-down" to karate contests, whereby a bout ended when one of the fighters was actually felled. His system allows for all-out strikes to the head and body by foot or by fist, and is a severe test for any karate-ka. The only contact prohibited is face contact. A tie is resolved by comparing the power generated by the two competitors when breaking blocks of wood.

Like the jeet kune-do kung-fu system of Bruce Lee, Oyama's method is not traditionally closed but contains elements of many fighting skills, from all over the world.

Moreover, as an example of the importance he places on esoteric exercises as an adjunct to martial arts training, Oyama once conducted an unusual experiment involving two of his students. For six months, one was called upon to train in the conventional pattern—using calisthenics and hand-hardening techniques, while the other concentrated solely on meditation and breathing techniques to tone his body. At the end of the period, the second student, who had done nothing in particular to harden his hands, could break as many bricks as his rival with a single blow, and had also developed a karate technique superior to the first.

A form of meditation is, in fact, used in all accredited karate dojos, usually related to the tenets (or nontenets!) of Zen Buddhism. This experience of meditation in the practice of karate, plus the experience of the ki force released when using the karate kiai shout of power, helps nudge the premier Japanese version of the martial arts firmly into the category of mystical arts—much in the way of its Chinese forerunners and/or counterparts.

The art of energy conversion

In Eastern terms, the seeming magick of the martial arts is generally considered to be made possible through direct operation of the mystical, primeval ch'i force; which, in its essence, relates primarily to internal power—as opposed to the external power of pure physical strength. It is that universal force which activates all beings and permeates all things, something like the Hindu *prana*, and the Tibetan *lung-oom*. On a more personal level, ch'i can be aligned with the Hindu concept of shakti or spirit energy. Richard

Wilhelm provides what may be termed closest to an acceptable definition of an indefinable concept in his translation of *The Secret of the Golden Flower* (New York: Harvest Books, 1970):

> Even if man lives in the energy (vital breath) he does not see the energy, just as fishes live in water but do not see the water. Man dies when he has not vital breath, just as fishes perish when deprived of water.

There is an astounding instance recorded on film of a display by Master Ueshiba Morihei, founder of the patently esoteric martial arts form known as *aikido* (see Chapter 5), which defies all known laws of time, space and bodily motion. A frame by frame replay reveals the then 75-year-old being charged from each side at top speed by a pair of judo black belts. In one frame, Master Ueshiba is seen to stand serene, waiting for his attackers as they are about to pounce on him; in the immediate next frame he is seen to be a distance away from his initial position, with his attackers about to collide head on! Thus, between two frames, in a time space of about one-eighteenth of a second, he has moved several feet, a demonstration which would be dubbed "impossible" if it were not for the fact that it has been filmed.

As another example of the apparently impossible made possible, respected Australian sportswriter Jeff Wells once described an amazing encounter with a Chinese-born t'ai ch'i master named Huang Sheng Shyan. Master Huang first received training in the Shaolin k'ung fu tradition, and then learned t'ai ch'i from one Cheng Man Ching, a professor of literature, who was also a master of other essential elements of the full t'ai ch'i experience, such as poetry, painting, calligraphy, meditation, and herbal medicine. In what he records as being "the closest thing I've had to a mystical experience," Wells tells of a display during which the slightly built, 80-year-old Huang (". . . this creaky old guy in pyjamas, who reminded me of an ancient barber who gave me atrocious haircuts in Hong Kong") easily subdued several opponents much his junior: "Men came at him, there was a sleight of hand and a caress, and suddenly they were either on their bums or flying across the room." (*The Weekend Australian*, April 15–16, 1989.)

In one instance, using the power of "ch'i," Huang appeared to knock over an assailant without even touching him. The explanation was that he had simply "killed" the other man's energy field. In what might be termed an interesting practical definition for a near-magickal performance, Wells refers to Huang's display as "the art of energy conversion," a definition which can also be used to describe the feats of Ueshiba, Oyama, Bruce Lee, and others. This art of energy conversion is also, of course, what "magick," as we know it in the West, is all about.

3 ☯ The power of ch'i

Great is the power of Ch'ien (primal creativity),
The source of all things, it embodies the
significance of Heaven. Clouds move and rain falls,
and all things develop in their appropriate forms.

I Ching

The hsin (mind) mobilizes the ch'i

Wu Yu-hsiang

Obey the nature of things,
and you are in concord with the Way.

Seng-t'san
On believing in the mind

The amazing feats demonstrated by Masters Huang
Sheng Shyan, Ueshiba Morihei, and others provide some
indication of the almost paranormal practical results that
might be achieved by an individual who masters any technique available to directly facilitate utilization of the ch'i
energy which permeates all aspects of our physical world.

In any of the martial arts, the development of
strength, stability, and poise comes about as a result of an

emphasis in training on correct stance development, a distinctly physical operation. In the generation of ch'i energy, however, the martial artist will rely on such seemingly esoteric practices as breathing exercises and meditation. The result can be far more potent than mere physical force.

In martial arts training, emphasis on stance development results in the development of strength, stability, and poise; to develop ch'i, the martial artist relies on such esoteric practices as breathing exercises and meditation. The result is far more potent than mere physical force.

The unfathomable Wu ch'i

In his *Tao and Longevity*, the prolific philosopher/author Huai-chin Nan presents a definition of ch'i based on the individual interpretations of the three Chinese characters used to portray its meaning—the characters representing: 1. "no-thing" plus "fire"; 2. "air in nature"; 3. "air, breath, or gas." It is interesting to note that Soviet psychic researchers have, in recent years, acknowledged the existence of ch'i energy, as utilized by the Master Huang, referring to it as "bio-plasmic energy." They hesitate, however, to call this energy "psychic," referring to it as electrical-type empirical energy, which may be a case of empirical hair-splitting. Perhaps one day science will come to recognize that the so-called supernatural as merely an extension of natural forces.

The Chinese association with the principles of ch'i energy goes back thousands of years. As one important example: it is central to the study of that profound Chinese guide to life known as *I Ching*. Tradition tells us that the eight basic symbols or trigrams of this "Oracle of

Changes" were initial-
ly discovered by Pao
Hsi, or Fu Hsi, great
Emperor of China,
some 4,800 years ago,
when he was contem-
plating the bright pat-
terns in the sky, the
shapes of the earth, the
decorative markings
on beasts and birds
and the peculiarities of
their territories, plus
his own body and dis-
tant things. The *I*

**The I Ching embodying the
symbol of Yin and Yang.**

Ching, with its emphasis on the countless permutations
found in the interaction of the forces of yin (female, earth)
and yang (male, heaven), is used to this day, in both East
and West, as a philosophical and spiritual guide and, in
an immediately practical application, as a divinatory tool.
The opening lines of the first of its 64 "hexagrams," as
quoted above, refers directly to the "source of all things,"
or "Ch'ien."

To understand ch'i further, it is necessary to have
some grasp of the essence of the cosmogony known as Tao
(literally "Way" and pronounced "da-o" or "dow"). The
legendary founder of Tao, the great sage Lao-tzu—whose
name means, literally, "The Old Master"—is frequently
depicted in ancient Chinese art riding a water buffalo.
This famous sixth century B.C.E. ascetic was thus very
familiar with the properties of running water: how when
it runs unimpeded, it remains fresh and clear; and when
there is a blockage in the river, the water soon becomes

stagnant and a breeding place for disease. According to many religious philosophies, all that occurs on the physical level, and within ourselves (the microcosm), is but a reflection of the heavens, the universe (the macrocosm). In Taoist tradition, the ch'i energy that courses through our bodies is seen much like water running in a river, either clear and safe, or muddy and stagnant. The key to unimpeded flow is, of course, the general condition of the individual's body, mind, and spirit.

There is an interesting contrast existing between the way of Tao and the Middle-Eastern Hebrew tradition that has so influenced the Western World. The Taoist is essentially "led by an Image to listen for a Voice," while the follower of the Hebrew tradition is "led by a Voice to conform to an Image."* The reason behind this difference in conceptual approach may be found in the fact that the Hebrew written language (and all Western written languages) consists of symbols representing individual sounds that, strung together, invoke an image, while in the Chinese language each written symbol is an ideographic presentation representing a complete statement, a visible image in itself (although it must be added that, in the deeper Kabbalistic sense, each of the Hebrew letters is taken to represent a total, individual concept). Deeper study of this linguistic phenomenon may one day lead the citizens of our world, Occidental and Oriental, toward understanding each other more effectively.

An old taoist story tells of a meeting between an aging Lao-tzu and another of China's major philosophers, Confucius, who was then already 51 years old, but had

---

* Lagerwey, John, *Taoist Ritual in Chinese Society and History* (New York: Macmillan Publishing Company, 1987), p. 283.

Lao-tzu

not yet experienced Tao. On being queried by Lao-tzu as to where he had been seeking Tao, Confucius answered that he had spent five years seeking it in the science of numbers, with no result; and then another twelve years seeking for it in the doctrine of yin and yang, still without success. Lao-tzu shook his wise old head and told the younger man: "Unless there is suitable endowment within, Tao will not abide; unless there is outward correctness, Tao will not operate."

Lao-tzu's concept of Tao is all-embracing; it is the originator and sustainor, "the mother of all things," the unfathomable, unnameable emptiness from which all creation springs—known in Chinese as the *Wu ch'i*.

In his epic *Tao te-Ching* (an oral tradition put into writing around the third century B.C.E.), Lao-tzu states: "Not to know the invariable, to act blindly, is to go to disaster." This statement echoes quite audibly the fundamental principles behind the work of kabalists, practitioners of magick, alchemists and the like, of many cultures. Knowledge is considered a necessity in order to guide correct action. Taking things a step further, Lao-tzu also insisted on naturalness in all actions—that human being and nature were both parts of an essential whole, and inextricably linked. The laws of the cosmos operating within the physical sphere affect equally man/woman and all of the kingdoms—animal, vegetable, mineral, and etheric. Attainment of harmony with the outside world thus leads to personal contentment. However, according to Tao, the individual human is incapable of grasping the Unnameable (God), or of fully understanding the beginning and ending of our cosmic existence.

The easiest method of understanding Tao is through the symbolism contained in the perfect circle of

Confucius

yin and yang. Where the beginning meets the end, the end is also the beginning. Everything in nature consists of two equal parts, yin and yang. In each is the seed of its opposite, and by their complimentary reaction all things exist. Permeating and interpenetrating all is the force known as ch'i. The human individual possesses virtually unlimited powers, but must learn how to stay in contact with these powers.

Tao and magick

Magick in its many forms was always an integrated part of Taoistic life in ancient China. Taoist doctors used both conventional methods and such useful adjuncts as astrology, magic spells, and talismans in their healing (their use of acupuncture was also considered magickal). *Fu-shui* "symbol-water," played an important part in banishing-type rituals. The geomantic phenomenon known as *feng shui*, the "dragon line" energy of the Earth itself (known in the West as ley lines), was (and still is) equated with the energy meridians of the human body, with each flowing through and affecting the other. The relationship of the traditional North American people, the Australian Aborigines, the Kalahari Bushmen of Africa, and other aboriginal folk of our planet, with the earth and nature itself (herself?) are all part of this process of inseparable interconnection and interaction between human being and living cosmos.

The Eastern view of science differs markedly from that of the West. What may be considered by the latter as mere magickal trickery or quackery is happily incorporated into an all-embracing Oriental system that acknowledges both the seen and the unseen. For the Occidental scientist, nature, by and large, is there to be exploited; for the Taoist, nature exists to be worked with, with the human being seen as not separate, but as an integrated part of the whole, affected by the whole. Thus, every action taken that harms nature will eventually reverberate in some damaging form against the person who takes such an action.

The fact of the matter is that traditional, tried and proven Chinese medicine is millenniums old, while its Western counterpart is an infant in comparison, and may well be described as the actual "alternative" medicine.

A striving for balance remains central to most Oriental thought and practices, including those of healing, martial arts practice, and the very human activity of sexual coupling. In the East, the belief still remains that sex plays a large part in the correct channeling of ch'i, and that an appropriately planned and executed union of female and male, negative and positive, yin and yang, contributes directly toward the harmony of the universe itself. It is even considered that there occurs an actual mini-consummation of the Heaven/Earth relationship each time a man and a woman perform a sexual act together. Thus, the Taoist practice of sex is seen very much in the same way as that of the practitioner of Tantra yoga rituals of higher union, whose prime aim is not mere sexual gratification but an opening-up of mystical awareness.

Overall, the prime goal of any Taoist magician was (and still is) the attainment of a state of "Oneness with the Universe," resulting in total spontaneity in action, and eventual dispensing with the need for any props or rituals. This should ideally, of course, be the ultimate goal for any magician, or person on any spiritual path, Eastern or

Western—i.e., the ability to spontaneously invoke whatever spiritual energies or forces are needed at any given moment without consciously thinking about how to invoke those forces, or taking any visible action to do so.

Other than the use of astrology, talismans, and magic spells, Taoist healers—and this would have included martial arts exponents, who were well known for their healing capabilities—frequently called upon the so-called "Spirits of the Prior Heavens" for assistance. Rituals were used in particular to invoke the energies of the Five Primordial Spirits connected with the five positions, namely: Fu Hsi for the East, Shao-hao for the West, Chuan-hsu for the North, Shen Hung for the South, and Huang-ti for the Center. It is interesting to note here that, against the Western tradition of four cardinal points to the compass, the Chinese always stressed the need for a fifth, balancing position, in the center of their global/spirit world map.

This fifth, central power, as used in ceremonial protection and other rituals, is, of course, fully acknowledged and utilized by many Western practitioners of Wicca and magick, normally in the form of an invocation of "spirit." In Wicca, for example, this is done by calling down the blessings of the God and Goddess in the center as the final part of an act of "preparing a place" through formation of a "circle," in which the elements of "fire," "water," "air," and "earth" are used, plus invocation of the protective powers of various "guardians" (spirits, elemental powers, Archangels, Watchtowers—depending on the tradition) at the four quarters. Variations include activation of the chakras of the Priest or Priestess concerned, or even of the entire group gathered in the center. This can be done, for example, by using a form of the well-known Kabalistic Middle Pillar exercise, in which the Higher Self and its connection with the God and Goddess is invoked. The Priest/Priestess (and, in some cases, the other participants) thus becomes a channel for the interplay of Heavenly and Earthly forces.

A reference to five-point balancing may also be contained in some of the Western Freemasonry rituals, in which the circle and the square play such an important role. As an example, according to Richard Carlile's *Manual of Freemasonry*,* the four corners of any Freemasons' lodge are generally connected with the principles of Temperance, Fortitude, Prudence, and Justice, while in the Third Degree Initiation of a Master Mason, it transpires that "ancient brethren" were taken into the "middle chamber of King Solomon's Temple" to receive their "wages."

Correspondences

It may be of some interest to Western practitioners of Wicca and the like, by way of change, to try developing and using a preparation ritual invoking the Chinese Five Primordial Spirits noted above, as related to the five cardinal positions and the five elements. For guidance, a table of essential correspondences (taken from the *Nei Ching* and other texts) for use in formulating such a ritual is given on the next page:

_____

* London: William Reeves (undated), p. 22; p. 63.

Table of Essential Correspondences

	East	South	Center	West	North
Primordial Spirits	Fin Hsi	Shen Nung	Huang-ti	Shao-hao	Chuan-hsu
Elements	wood	fire	earth	metal	water
Color	green	red	yellow	white	black
Seasons	Spring	Summer	between seasons	Fall	Winter
Number	8	7	5	9	6
Planet	Jupiter	Mars	Saturn	Venus	Mercury
Animal	fowl	sheep	ox	horse	pig
Basic energy	psychic	motivating	primal	physical	creative
Spiritual	benevolence	righteousness	tranquility	religious fervor	wisdom
Climate	windy	hot	humid	dry	cold

(Note: some other correspondences are given on the following pages—
see "Many types of ch'i.")

The Confucianist influence

In ancient China, the Taoists and the Confucianists (followers of the teachings of Confucius) were, in their opposition of ideas, something like the Biblical Pharisees and Sadducees. Notwithstanding the totally unjustifiable and negative image portrayed of them in the New Testament, the Pharisees were a vibrant, charismatic sect, the forerunners of the mystical Jewish Hassidim, who reveled in the existence of the spirit life. The Sadducees, on the other hand, were dry-as-dust fundamental believers in the written Law, who denied the concepts of immortality and the spiritual world. Both groups were, however, Jewish, and this was their common link. In a curious ancient Chinese parallel, the Taoist happily moved along his way of intuitive magick, while the Confucianist chose to observe the strictures imposed by ritual, ceremony, and preordained social order. In effect, the Taoist, with a whole pantheon of gods and goddesses to relate to, and in a general attitude of gaiety and enjoyment of life, represented the yin energy force. The rather puritanical Confucianist epitomized the more sobering yang influence. A curious synthesis of the two virtually opposite attitudes to the scheme of things was apparently achieved via a mutual awareness and acknowledgement of the power of the all-encompassing ch'i, albeit from slightly different viewpoints.

Although the patriarchal and proper Confucianists accepted the existence of ch'i and its overriding importance, they taught that ch'i itself was subservient to an even higher principle called l'i. To become in tune with this l'i force it was necessary to lead a totally controlled and virtuous life.

The end result in a mixed Taoist/Confucianist society, with overtones of Buddhism to make things even more interesting, manifested in the usual Oriental sense of balance.

Many types of ch'i

In the Chinese context, ch'i can take on many and varied forms, relating to various aspects of life, such as health, work, art, philosophical practice, science, magick, the martial arts, and even town planning. There are, for example, at least six types of ch'i related to health and healing. Using English terminology, these refer to:

♦ **primal or original ch'i:** nutritional energy derived by way of the kidneys through food, drink, and oxygen.

♦ **organic ch'i:** ch'i subsisting in the human body as a harmonizing factor controlling the bodily organs.

♦ **circulatory ch'i:** related to the meridian energy system throughout the body that can be stimulated or corrected through the use of acupuncture needles.

♦ **blood ch'i:** carried by the blood and also derived from food and drink; the supplier of nutrients to the body and an internal defense system against disease.

♦ **electromagnetic ch'i:** this form of protective energy operates just beyond the surface of the physical body, regulating body temperature; associated with the concept of the aura.

♦ **vital energy ch'i:** related to the respiratory system and the heart cardiac function; controls physical stamina.

Ch'i emanating from the original universal source is referred to as yuan ch'i. Special names for other types of ch'i include: jing ch'i (bioelectrical energy of the body); k'ing ch'i (energy from the atmosphere); gu ch'i (energy from food); wei ch'i (protective energy).

The written Chinese character for ch'i is a "picture" of steam rising from a pot of cooking rice. Thus, in its simplest meaning, ch'i relates to the energy derived from food. However, the rising steam also indicates a connection with the breath. In the Chinese tradition, ch'i is also tied in with the five phases of physical energy evolution, namely, earth, metal, water, wood, and fire—each being a symbol for various phenomena in nature, and related to the five points of the magickal pentagram, symbol for the microcosm. (By adding a mystical sixth element—i.e, the essence of all the other five taken together, the six-pointed interlaced triangles of the Solomonic or Davidic star can be invoked as the symbol of the macrocosm.) The five elements system is used alongside the *I Ching* to help explain the nature of our world and the cosmos—as a sort of Chinese Kabbalah, equatable to some degree with the wisdom of the Tree of Life of the Middle East sages, numerology and other corresponding systems. All elements are totally inter-related in a continual stream of life—fire burns wood; the resultant ashes mingle with earth, which produces metal; when melted metal turns to water. Some basic correspondences are (see also "Correspondences" above):

Table of Essential Correspondences

	Wood	Fire	Earth	Metal	Water
Organs	liver gall- bladder	heart small intestine	spleen stomach	lungs large intestine	kidneys bladder
Tissues	ligaments	arteries	muscles	skin/hair	bones
Orifices	eyes	ears	nose	mouth	anal
Sense	sight	taste	touch	smell	hearing
Flavor	sour	bitter	sweet	spicy	salty
Emotion	anger	joy	reflection	grief	fear

Feng shui

The practice of *feng shui* (literally "wind/water"), or Chinese earth magick, is part and parcel of the ch'i concept of all parts of the universe being connected in some subtle and mysterious way. This idea follows in part the famous "chaos theory," which makes the allegorical assertion that the flapping of a butterfly's wings somewhere in the Amazon forest could initiate a direct effect on seismological movement in another part of the planet. According to feng shui practitioners, everything animate and inanimate—mountains, rocks, trees, rivers, the sea, and people—breathe inward and outward constantly, affecting each other, and being themselves affected, not only by their own breathing actions, but by the very cosmos itself.

Thus, feng shui experts are called in whenever a new building is to be constructed, a roadway is to be designed, a new business commenced, or a couple are preparing for marriage. They will help to choose the most appropriate site, usually where the dragon or ley lines conjunct harmoniously, or set the most propitious date, when, according to the feng shui master's calculations, all the forces of Heaven and Earth will be at their most beneficent. The feng shui geomancy expert can map both the ch'i currents in the human body and the ch'i currents flowing through any particular area of the Earth's surface, and match these up with such other essential data as contained in astrological charts and the like. The invisible ch'i currents of the Earth are known as "dragon's veins" and are determined not only by the position of sea, river, mountain, or valley, but by the positions of the stars in the sky at any given moment in time.

These ch'i flow currents can be either yin or yang in nature, and can change from one to the other, from time to time. If a proposed building site is considered to be placed in a position generating unsuitable ch'i, construction may be delayed for months, or even years, until the ch'i current changes to a more favorable aspect. Above and below ground water courses are natural carriers of ch'i and it is sometimes advised that the course of a river or canal be altered, sometimes only very slightly, to take advantage of "good ch'i" vibrations. As the dragon is considered (in feng shui terms) the most propitious of animal forms, it is always considered fortunate to be located close to a hill or mountain shaped like a dragon.

In Eastern countries, the dragon is associated with wealth, prosperity, and social success, representing the yin principle of creation. The yang aspect is signified by the tiger. The ideal setting for home or business should embody a subtle interplay of the two forces. The so-called mating place of the "azure dragon" of the East and the "white tiger" of the West is considered to be a particularly ideal spot for perfect balancing of the ch'i energies.

In addition to ch'i, yin and yang, two other motivating principles play an important role in feng shui lore: l'i—the immutable law of the universe; so—the mathematical principle behind all creation.

Ch'i and the martial artist

In line with the principles of feng shui and other Chinese/Taoist magickal-type practices, martial arts exponents acquire control of the ch'i force primarily through a combination of breath control, body movement, and relaxation and meditation techniques that are, paradoxically, more in keeping with non-violent religious practices than with the development of fighting and self-defense techniques.

As is the case with human blood, ch'i travels throughout the body, to nourish and to maintain life, to rehabilitate failing physical health, and to recharge the human spirit. It can also be called upon, by those who know how to use it, as an instant power base for (to the uninitiated) seemingly miraculous physical feats. As it is an electrical type of energy, it uses the body's nervous system as a circuitry base. Ch'i is breath but more than breath. It is a vital and fundamental component of the universe, to be harnessed and used by an individual to overcome any attacker, even if the assailant be far more powerful in terms of pure physical strength than the one attacked.

It is believed in the East that total understanding of the essence of ch'i brings with it perfect health and mental control and complete spiritual enlightenment. Combined with exercise of the will, or *hsing-i,* the use of ch'i can also produce the more spectacular aspects of the martial arts, as seen in the breaking of stacks of bricks, or the withstanding of normally killer blows, or in "killing" an opponent's energy field, as already discussed. This "magickal aspect" of mind over matter is also evident in such essentially shamanistic practices as fire-walking and the cutting and skewering of parts of the human body without drawing blood or causing any scar—all of which have also been demonstrated by certain martial arts experts from time to time.

Another special aspect of the ch'i principle, more related to the actual organic growth of life-forms, is known as *jing* (essence). The basic ch'i and jing in the universe are, however, mutually interdependent, and are also closely related to the principle termed *shen*—the spirit of primal consciousness, or the soul whose presence can be seen shining out through the eyes of each and every person.

It remains relevant to state that it is generally accepted in the East that in its ultimate form any martial arts system should ideally aim at the development of the ability to react not in a personal way, with anger or ambitious intent, but as if in fulfillment of a natural law. It follows therefore that the most important exercises in any martial arts curriculum must relate directly to the cultivation and control of the all-pervading ch'i energy. Moreover, there can be little doubt that this is best achieved not only through concentrated physical exercise (which remains, however, necessary), but also through serious study of the philosophical roots behind the fighting arts, and through a predetermined spiritual practice, usually involving some form of meditation.

T'ai ch'i and Wu ch'i

Wang Tsung-yueh, first known successor to Chang San-feng, acknowledged founder of the martial arts style we now know as *t'ai ch'i chaun*, writes in his classic *T'ai Ch'i*

Ch'uan Lun: "T'ai ch'i comes from Wu ch'i and is the mother of yin and yang." This profound statement establishes an immediate supernatural credential for what is one of the most paradoxical of all the Eastern martial arts forms. Wang Tsung-yueh is referring, of course, to the evolution of the cosmos from its primordial state (wu ch'i) into two antithetical forces, yin and yang—through the agency of t'ai ch'i.

For the record, tai means "grand," and ch'i "ultimate," which, if taken literally, makes t'ai ch'i chuan "grand ultimate fist" or "grand ultimate martial art form." It is also, without doubt, one of the more esoteric and mystical of the oriental combat skills. T'ai ch'i's slow, graceful movements can be observed at dawn, lunch-break, and at dusk in just about every park and open space around the world, wherever there is a Chinese community. For many it is considered solely as a highly popular method of physical exercise, to relax and tone the muscles, improve blood circulation and regulate breathing.

In its ultimate, speeded-up form, however, t'ai ch'i is a method of boxing as skilled as (some say more skilled than) any other martial arts form. It is one of the four so-called "internal" or "soft school" Chinese martial arts, the *nei chia*. The soft school arts place special emphasis on the philosophical and/or metaphysical aspects of k'ung fu, over the more physical and forceful considerations of the external or hard school systems. Moreover, t'ai ch'i and the other "soft" arts remain firmly grounded in the Taoist philosophy of Lao-tzu, the thoughts of Confucius, and the concepts of yin and yang described earlier. In the words of Australia-based t'ai ch'i master, Tennyson Yiu, it is "the interplay of yin and yang, with the object of seeking serenity in action, and action in serenity."

T'ai chi's slow, graceful movements can be seen in almost every park in China.

As a typical example of this "action in serenity," in 1971, the already-mentioned master Huang Sheng Shyan, then still a sprightly 60-year-old, was seen to humiliate Malaysian wrestling champion Leow Kong Seng, who was half his age and almost twice his weight. The already mature t'ai ch'i master repeatedly threw his much younger opponent to the ground during a 15-minute contest, without once losing balance himself.

Inner and outer skills

It is held that in order to be adept at t'ai ch'i, it is essential to develop both inner and outer skills. The t'ai ch'i symbol tells it all: the complete, integrated circle, indicating no starting and no ending point. Where t'ai ch'i differs very much from some of the other martial arts systems is in the fact that, generally, a student is first taught to master the slower, exercise-oriented movements (as a form of physical and mental exercise stimulating the philosophical/spiritual approach), before any emphasis is placed on learning defense/attack skills. In some systems, the norm is to allow the philosophical to develop out of the combative.

The metaphysical objective in t'ai ch'i is to bring the mind and body into perfect harmony. Its philosophy is rooted within the principles of yin and yang, as well is in the similar *wu-wei* concept of Taoism. Wu-wei, like yin and yang, represents the principles of non-action and action and leads to a spontaneous reaction to an attacking situation rather than a conscious preparation for defense.

Success in t'ai ch'i is also, of course, dependent at all times on an understanding of the flow of the all-pervading ch'i force.

Of three other major soft school, or nei chia, k'ung fu systems (in addition to t'ai ch'i chuan), the graceful *hsing-i chuan* is, for the serious student, a form of moving Zen that leads to an understanding of the secrets of the physical form, until its practice eventually transcends technique and enters the realm of the metaphysical, where all the secrets of the entire cosmos become clear. The other two soft school arts—*liou-ho-pa-fa* and *pa-kau chang*—also embody body/mind and mind/spirit connotations and, as is the case with t'ai ch'i and hsing-i, are firmly based in Taoist magick. All combine the principles of inner strength (ch'i), the spirit of power (sheng), the ultimate creative principle (win ch'i) and the Taoist concept of ultimate stillness (yuan ch'i).

Shout of power

In Japan, ch'i power is known as ki, although there is no ideal English translation for the Japanese word *kiai*—the expression representing the "shout of power" exhaled when making a move or strike, an act which serves to personify in particular the karate exponent, and which is used in some form or another in most other martial arts systems. Interestingly, the closest translation might be something like "spirit meeting." The violent exhalation of air in the form of a shout just before or during an attack is designed to bring strength to the body and to inure it against the effects of a blow. It reflects an attempt to balance spiritual resolve and physical action and thus provide the correct impetus for a selected movement.

Use of the power of sound, or of "the word," has long been a central theme in ancient esoteric texts. Even today, around the world, shamans and medicine folk, from the sangomas of Africa to the kahunas of Hawaii, use sound as an essential part of their power system. As one example only, the Kahuna magician-priests of Hawaii possess a system of ritual and vocalized magic which enables them to heal the sick, communicate telepathically, astral project, forecast the future, and control the weather. Through vocalization of the so-called *Ha* prayer (similar in sound to the Japanese kiai shout), the Hawaiian medicine person is able to contact intangible worlds for assistance and inspiration and, in extreme cases, even invoke the dreaded "death prayer" to perhaps rid his particular island of an enemy or other undesirable person.

Kiai, the shout of power as employed in the martial arts context, is used as a focusing technique. It originates in the diaphragm, and is forced up to the throat by the muscles of the lower abdomen, the area of the body which is thought to be the source of all power, known in Japanese as the *hara*, the ki/ch'i energy point just below the navel. Out of the use of the kiai shout comes a gathering of all the energy forces of the body, the mind, and the spirit, in a coordinated effort known as *kime*. Fighting arts masters claim that they are able to sense the level of *kokyu* (a Japanese word indicating level of ability in use of ki/ch'i energy) possessed by any of their pupils.

In addition to its mystical connotations, on an immediately practical level, the kiai shout helps to tighten the abdominal muscles, in a way and at a point in time critical to the required physical exertion. Apart from perhaps scaring the adversary, it also helps to get the tongue out of the way, which can be inadvertently bitten during the intense moment of concentration surrounding a strike.

Legend tells us that the kiai energy can be used to stun a small animal or bird with one yell, and then to revive the creature again with another shout. It has been claimed that a Japanese practitioner of traditional medicine is even able to cure a nose-bleed using the power of the kiai shout. Other claims include the one that true masters of the art can summarily render an opponent unconscious with a shout that is heard by others in the vicinity, but not by the person under attack. There have been suggestions that this method of *kiai-jiutsu* may in actual fact be some form of hypnotism. The fact probably is that few pragmatic martial artists pay much attention to the mystical aspects of the kiai utterance, but all acknowledge its practical physiological values. As martial arts instructor Tom Crone has so succinctly pointed out to us, even tennis players are now becoming famous for their "grunts."

Within our human heritage there is a vast storehouse of magickal words, mantras, invocations, and chants handed down through the ages. The ancients used these sacred sounds to still the mind, heal the body and attain higher states of consciousness. It does not, therefore, seem out of place at all that martial arts masters, whose primary aim is to spiritualize themselves and their students, should utilize in their teachings such useful legacies from our forebears. (We have elsewhere enlarged on the theme of use of specified sounds for controlled purposes and direct interested readers to our book *Words of Power: Sacred Sounds of East and West* [St. Paul, Llewellyn Publications], 1991.)

The well-known South African karate master, Stan Schmidt, has recommended his pupils use a specific Japanese phrase as a shout of power—"shu ha ri." Translated literally, this would mean something like: "master-express-next." When expressing the word "shu," the karateka's master should be visualized; "ha" refers to the self; and "ri" takes the karateka into the next dimension of reality—the ideal state to be in for perfect control of all fighting and associated faculties.

As a final note of interest, one of the more esoteric and magickal of the martial arts, the Japanese *aikido* (see Chapter 5), bears in its name a concept that is the opposite of kiai in form and intention. The kiai shout, in essence, helps direct energy of a mental, physical, and/or psychical nature. Aiki-do means "way of harmony with universal energy," indicating control of the ki/ch'i by spiritual forces, and not merely physical or psychical energy.

4 ☯ The gateless gate

To action alone hast thou the right but never to the fruits thereof. Be thou neither motivated by the fruits of action nor be thou attached to inaction.

Lord Krishna
Srimad Bhagavad Gita

A journey of a thousand miles must begin with a single step.

Lao-tzu
Tao te-Ching

The Perfect Way knows no difficulties
Except that it refuses to make preference.

Seng-ts'an
On believing in mind

In every Japanese martial arts dojo, and in many other martial arts training halls in East and West, there hangs in a special place a portrait of a rather ferocious-looking individual with spaced-out front teeth. Known as Dharuma to the Japanese, Bodhidharma to the Chinese, he is, as we have already recorded, the almost universally acknowledged "patron saint" of the martial arts. And if

51

the legends about this crusty old character are to be accepted, the martial arts as practiced today did actually have their origin in India.

Bodhidharma, so legend tells us, was born the third child of an Indian king, Sughanda. He was a member of the feared Indian warrior caste, the *Kshatriya*, and spent his early years in Kancheepuram, a Buddhist province in South India. There he trained to become a warrior, but later became a monk. Venerated as the 28th reincarnation of Gautama Buddha, he is reputed to have crossed the seemingly impassable Himalayas on foot, to bring *Ch'an* or *Zen Buddhism*, an offshoot of Mahayana Buddhism, to China around 527 C.E. Ch'an in Chinese means meditation, and comes from the Indian/Tibetan Sanskrit word *Dhyana*, the root of which is *dhyai*, "to meditate."

The basic difference between Mahayana/Zen Buddhism and, for instance, the teachings of Indian Hinduism, is that the former contends that all persons possess the "buddha nature," while the latter states that the Atman, the individual soul/spirit, is identical with Brahman, or God. Zen is also connected with the Chinese Tao philosophy in its insistence on using the intuitive processes, but is itself neither a philosophy, as such, nor a religion. It propounds no dogmas, nor beliefs, and has no set symbols, temples, or monastic vows, in the usual religious sense. All that is carried forward in Zen tradition are the *koan*, the "stories" of the Zen masters that illustrate its curiously enigmatic essence. The principle objective in Zen is to find sudden enlightenment (in Japanese, *satori*) through meditation, rather than through assiduous study and ritualistic practice, as in most other traditions.

Listening to the ants scream

Bodhidharma (known to the Chinese as Ta-mo), in addition to his Zen teachings, is also alleged to have carried with him to the Shaolin temple and monastery at the foot of the Songshan Mountains in the Kingdom of Wei (now the northern Chinese province of Hunan), a system of yoga exercises. These he used to aid his brother monks in upgrading their poor physical condition, the result of hours of motionless meditation.

The story goes that, after his arrival at the Shaolin monastery, Bodhidharma himself sat in silent meditation, facing the wall of his cave retreat, for a full nine years— "listening to the ants scream." During this time he devised and perfected both his Zen Buddhism and special yoga system, which consisted of a set of breathing techniques, plus physical exercises."

Legend also reveals that this former Indian warrior-turned-monk provided his new-found colleagues with a third gift—a unique method of self-defense called *i-chin-ching*. This form of weaponless martial arts was probably derived from what he had learned as a young member of the Indian Kshatriya warrior caste. There has never been much advertisement of the Indian sub-continent's various unarmed combat techniques, many of which are quite as effective as their more well-known Chinese and/or Japanese counterparts. Countries like Malaysia, Burma, Indonesia, and the Philippines have produced a wide variety of fighting forms, similar in content to those found elsewhere in Asia. In India, Bodhidharma's original home, one of the most intriguing of all martial arts systems has been practiced for many hundreds of years. Known as *kalaripayit*, its features vary from the spectacular high leaps and kicks of the so-called "northern style" to the more solid circular blocking movements of the "southern style."

More importantly, and in keeping with a supposition that we will propose later—i.e., that there is a defined link between movement and contact with the "inner self"—many of the kalaripayit postures simulate or suggest those found in classical Indian dance, which has its own roots set firmly in the soil of traditional Indian magickal/spiritual practice—and which, most likely, also carries some esoterically linked influences from the Middle East and Egypt.

Bodhidharma's i-chin-chang later developed into the martial arts system known as *shih-pa Lo Han sho*—eighteen hands of the Lo Han (the Lo Han being the 500 disciples of Buddha who had achieved Nirvana and were themselves destined to return to Earth as Buddhas). It is now known more simply as *Lohan-k'ung* and was later extended from 18 movements to 72 movements, and then to 173 movements, to form the basis of *Shaolin chuan-fa* (temple boxing), which system, carrying with it its already mentioned Indian influences, has so greatly influenced all subsequent branches of the martial arts throughout Asia, and ultimately, the rest of the world.

For himself, Bodhidharma remains something of a shadowy enigma. Only one written account mentions him directly, that of Yang Hsuan-chih, in 547 C.E. (Yang Hsuan-chih records the claim by Bodhidharma to be 150 years old, and that he had traveled to many kingdoms). After this account, nothing is heard about the founder of the martial arts in any text until some 500 years later. With the burning of the original Shaolin monastery records in 1928, all chance of finding further references have virtually been lost. Moreover, Bodhidharma may not have been the only Indian martial arts adept to cross over the Himalayas into China. Several historical paintings picture Indian and Chinese pugilists squaring up to each other. It has also been claimed that the famous Shaolin monastery was originally built for another Indian monk, Fo Tuo (or Batuo), by the Chinese Emperor Hsaio-wen. The statue of Fo Tuo depicting a huge-bellied, laughing monk can be seen in many Chinese monasteries and has been copied world-wide as a good luck ornament in many homes. (Fo Tuo is also probably the role model for the exceedingly popular Japanese God of Good Fortune, Hotei-Osho.)

The magick of the Shaolin monks

It is a recorded fact that the original Shaolin monks were supporters of the Ming dynasty and were driven out of their monastery by the Manchus during the seventeenth century. This action by the Manchus resulted in the spread of the Shaolin methods of k'ung fu all over China. Regardless of whether k'ung fu actually originated within their order or not, it was the Shaolin monks who, over the centuries, first became feared and revered for their skill at unarmed combat. Under normal circumstances, and other than during warfare, the Shaolin monks would only strike a fatal blow in a life or death situation. An important feature of Shaolin k'ung fu is the salute, the ritual sign of respect and humility whereby the right fist of power is covered by the left fist to show that an individual is unarmed and without hostile intention; but the right fist is always at the ready if needed in self-defense.

The Shaolin warrior monks would, in times of emergency, frequently spearhead the attack for their emperor in local conflicts. After one famous victory the then Tang dynasty emperor Li Shih-min was so impressed by the Shaolin monks' fighting ability that he asked them all to become generals in his army. All but one of the warrior monks declined, asking instead to be allowed to continue with their devotions to Buddha. Emperor Li acceded to their wish and presented them each with a royal cloak. He also placed a commemorative tablet at the monastery, lauding the Shaolin monks' great valor in battle.

Their fabled abilities took on an almost magickal aura and, over and above their fighting prowess, they were considered great adepts in many other marvelous skills—such as miraculous healing, control over the weather, rendering themselves invisible, and even being able to fly. Modern movies made in Hong Kong and elsewhere frequently portray martial arts monks of ages past who are able to perform all of these feats with ease.

One especially famous early Shaolin master was the holy monk Hung Yun who, during the Ming dynasty, combined the elements of a number of martial arts systems at his eclectic school at Tien Shan Szu, the Celestial Mountain Monastery. His fighting monks were particularly noted for their tough resistance to the Manchurians and their Ch'ing dynasty. Hung Yun's martial arts method became known as *tien shan p'ai k'ung fu* and was an amalgam of several other fighting forms.

The Shaolin temple boxing tradition was speedily embraced by other monasteries and still existed almost a thousand years after Bodhidharma's passing. Shaolin chuan (Shaolin fist) continued to be used in times of emergency by the hundreds of itinerant monks who would wander alone the length and breadth of China seeking knowledge and enlightenment. The Shaolin tradition thus provided a blueprint for all the Chinese martial arts that followed.

There is, for the record, an alternative story about the origins of *chang chuan,* and therefore k'ung fu, which places its genesis at a much later date than the sixth century Shaolin story. This opposition legend tells of the birth and growth of the art of chang chuan during the reign of T'ai Tzu, first emperor of the Sung dynasty which ruled China between the years 960 and 976 C.E. Chang chuan is a fighting form characterized by wide open and sweeping arm and fist motions, low stances, and high kicks, much in the style of Northern Shaolin methods—as opposed to the Southern Shaolin style which favors hand strikes and punches. There is, indeed, an old saying among martial artists which offers a simple comparison between the two definite styles of k'ung fu developed in two separate parts of China: "The North kicks, the South punches."

Shamanistic and totemistic elements

The observation earlier that certain Shaolin monks were able to "fly" suggests a distinctive shamanistic connection, but relating possibly to an "out-of-body" type experience. Chinese lore abounds with stories of shamans and shamanesses able to "fly into heaven," meaning an ability to transcend the physical while in a state of ecstacy. Importantly, in our present context, according to the famous expert on world shamanism, Mircea Eliade: ". . . it is striking to observe the absence of references to 'possession' in the Chinese tradition of 'magical flight' and of the shamanic dance."* This places the Chinese out-of-body experience in a slightly different category from that of many shamans elsewhere, who generally depend on a type of "possession" for their ecstatic experiences. What is alluded to is that the Chinese shamans, and martial artists such as the Shaolin monks, were perhaps able to transcend the physical and operate on the intuitive/spiritual plane without being possessed or controlled by some normally discarnate entity.

The five major divisions of Shaolin or Chinese temple boxing are named for the five Shaolin monks reputed to have first developed them—Hung, Lau, Li, Choy and Monk. Out of these styles the art of modern k'ung fu developed. The expression k'ung fu means, simply, "hard work by someone at a special skill," the word "fu" meaning "man." The term "k'ung" has also taken on the connotation of "power" or "force." The basic Chinese fighting arts method is actually known in China as *chung-kuo chuan*, "Chinese fist or hand." An early version of the art was known simply as *chang chuan*. Moreover, individual fighting techniques evolved that were based on the subtle motions of various animals.

These movements became grouped into five distinct styles known as the *Five Animals Fist*. Separately they were called after the crane (stressing balance, the development of sinews, and quick, pecking hand motions); the dragon (spirit, agility, and grace); the leopard (physical power); the tiger (strengthening of bones, and short-range clawing movements); and the snake (control and striking

---

* *Shamanism: Archaic Techniques of Ecstasy,* translated from the French by Willard R. Trask (Princeton: Bollingen Press, 1964), p. 450.

at the right moment). Each of the five methods was devised through observation of the movements of the animals concerned. The k'ung fu practitioner is meant to identify completely with the creature whose style he/she is following.

Among ancient peoples of all the continents, symbolic animals and birds were considered as sent from the spirit world to guide and instruct humans. Shamans, the mediumistic medicine folk of the tribes, were acknowledged as being able to communicate freely with the totem spirits—which means that identification with the movements of any specified animal introduces a definitive totemistic element into the Shaolin-based martial arts. Moreover, when a martial artist uses meditation and other esoteric techniques in training, the methods of the ancient shaman are to a certain extent also simulated. Another parallel between martial arts practices and shamanism (i.e., magick) is in the area of mystical and other healing (see Chapter 11).

Several additional k'ung fu styles based on movements made by various creatures have been added over the years, with numerous legends attached to the origin of each. The praying mantis style, for example, was inspired by the battle witnessed by a seventeenth century k'ung fu master named Wong Long between a praying mantis and a grasshopper, in which the former insect used clear-cut strategy and technique to out-fight his opponent. A Tibetan lama is reputed to have initiated the original white crane style by duplicating the movements made by a crane in its fight with an ape. The crane overcame its awesomely strong attacker by using its powerful wings for balance and poking repeatedly at weak spots in the ape's body. The ape eventually fled after one of its eyes had been pecked out. Another story places the origin of a crane style in the hands of a woman, Yim Wing Chun, who studied k'ung fu under a Buddhist nun, Mg Mui. Yim's innovation differs, however, from the Tibetan monk's purely crane style in that it embodies the fighting tactics of both a crane and a snake, which creatures she once observed fighting each other.

The snake style, as such, came reputedly from the so-called yang style of tai-ch'i chuan developed by the famous eleventh century alchemist and martial arts master, Chang San-feng, of the Mol Don monastery, after he had observed a fight between a crow and a snake. The snake, it is recorded, kept on evading the crow until the bird was exhausted, and then went in for its strike.

Imitating monkeys

Anyone who enters a *kwoon*, or training hall, where students of *ta-sheng pi-kua mern* are at work, and expects to see a demonstration of k'ung fu, might be readily excused if he were to think that he had taken the wrong turning and arrived instead at the monkey house in the local zoo. Ta-sheng pi-kua mern is named partly for Ta-sheng, the monkey god, and partly after a k'ung fu method called *ti-tang mern*, or grand earth method, and is a martial arts form well in keeping with the shamanistic/totemistic forms of fighting discussed above. Students of this unique martial arts style are encouraged to behave like monkeys, screeching, grabbing, falling, lunging, and jumping about, so that they may become infused with the qualities of agility and mobility possessed by that creature. The art of Ta-sheng also involves an element of

K'ung fu—the snake style.

deviousness, unpredictability and destructiveness, in tune with the nature of the monkey.

Today's acknowledged grandmaster of Ta-sheng pi-kau mern is Chan Sau Chung, who has his academy in Kowloon, Hong Kong. The style was founded in the early 1900s by one Kou Sze, a k'ung fu expert who had been imprisoned for murder after killing an assailant in self-defense. From his cell window, Kou Sze would daily observe a troop of monkeys on the outside. He began to incorporate their movements in his own k'ung fu technique, and later passed them on to his pupils after his release from prison.

A variation of Kou Sze's style is *ta-sheng pek kwa*, combining the agility of the monkey with the decisive hitting power of *pek kwa*, the k'ung fu ax-fist style founded a century before by the master Ma Chi Ho. As a young man, Ma Chi Ho was busy one day, chopping wood with an ax in each hand, when a passing Taoist monk remarked that "metal may conquer wood but the spirit conquers all." The thoughtful Ma interpreted this remark as meaning that he should dispense with his ax. He did so and was amazed to find that he was able to chop wood effectively with his bare fist and thus was born the k'ung fu system called pek kwa.

Hard and soft—yin and yang

As a direct reflection of the yin/yang, positive/negative principle found back of most aspects of existence in the East, k'ung fu, early on, became divided into two distinct schools: the so-called external "hard" (yang) schools which stress forceful power strikes, hand and body conditioning, and kicking (Shaolin chuan-fa or Shaolin fist; hung gar chuan; tong long); and the internal "soft" (yin) schools (pa-kau; hsing-i; t'ai ch'i chuan), which embody more of the metaphysical, philosophical, and magickal in their methodology. In accordance with yin principles, the internal schools are considered relatively passive, tending toward the spiritual; the yang-influenced external schools concentrate more on the muscular and aggressive approach. However, each contains certain very definable elements of the other.

The concepts of yin and yang may still remain something of a mystery for most Westerners, who tend to think of the world as one of black and white opposites striving for dominance over each another. Orientals, on the other hand, are more comfortable with the metaphysical ideal of inseparable opposing forces that are complimentary and interchangeable, and that flow unceasingly one into the other, as day flows into night and then back into day. Yin relates to the negative aspect of the universe (softness, night, female, the moon, immobility, etc.); yang to the positive aspect of the universe (fullness, the sun, hardness, male, mobility). Yin is the black, fish-shaped sector with the white eye in the yin-yang symbol; yang is the white fish with the black eye in the same familiar circular image.

But although, together, yin and yang are complementary, they are never fixed and immutable. According to Taoist philosophy, they are interchangeable—yin gradually becomes yang, and yang becomes yin. When either is in excess or deficiency, imbalance and disharmony may rule. When they are equal, all on Earth and in Heaven is in order.

The yin-yang principle pervades all thought in the East. Everything in the universe is either yin or yang, but neither is absolute. Every yin (negatively-charged) thing contains an element of yang and every yang (positively-charged) thing a measure of yin. Yin cannot exist without yang—and vice versa. Thus, when they are not in harmony, there exists imbalance, be it personal (of the body, mind, or spirit), or universal (of the personal relationship, social order, or universal philosophy). From a strictly personal viewpoint, the ideal is to achieve complete equality and accord of the yin and yang forces in all activities and attitudes.

The gateless gate

Notwithstanding the inconclusive evidence for the meditating monk, Bodhidharma, as founding father of the martial arts, there can be no contesting that one of the greatest philosophical/mystical influences behind the fighting arts (including the universally popular Japanese karate) has come from its Zen Buddhism component—Zen Buddhism having been, according to legend, brought to China by Bodhidharma. It may also be quite permissible to note that Zen practice, as it now stands, derives both from Indo/Tibetan Buddhism (as per Bodhidharma) and Taoism (as taught by Lao-Tzu and his disciples), with a touch of Confucianist influence for added spice.

The direct influence of Taoism on the martial arts will be discussed later—in particular in its relation to the ubiquitous "ch'i" force, and its links with ancient Chinese magickal practices. For itself, Zen, as a spiritual discipline with its base firmly planted in the practice of meditation, is almost impossible to define—simply because true Zen possesses no visible theory, and no apparent dogma. The ultimate Zen ideal has, however, been captured quite enchantingly (as much as it is possible to do so) by the Japanese teacher, Yoka Daishi, in his "Song of Enlightenment":

> Knowest thou that leisurely philosopher has gone beyond learning and is not exerting himself in anything? He neither endeavors to avoid idle thoughts nor seeks after truth;
>
> For he knows that ignorance in reality is the Buddha-nature.

The essence of elementary Zen—if it can ever be captured in words—is to emphasize intuitive response, and de-emphasize action based on intellectual judgment. This emphasis on the intuitive or subconscious response over conscious action certainly brings a sense of magick into those martial arts methods that rely upon Zen principles for their spiritual/philosophical base.

The celebrated Zen Buddhism "Ten ox-herding pictures" contained in the Manual of Zen Buddhism (a set of cartoons dating from the fifteenth century and said to be the work of a Chinese Zen master of the Sung Dynasty known as Kuo-an Shih-yuan) have for hundreds of years provided a model for use in the attaining of enlightenment along the Way of Zen—and go some way toward giving a clearer explanation of what Zen is all about. Contemplation of the allegorical principles contained in the ox-herding drawings may also be of some use to anyone practicing the martial arts, or who is involved in any one of the many spiritual cum magickal paths.*

In the first of the ten ox-herding pictures (titled "undisciplined") the black-colored ox (the unruly self) is noted running free over the mountain paths, with the oxherd standing helpless. Picture number two ("discipline begun") shows a rope placed through the beast's nose ring, and the oxherd using his whip as the ox resists training. The next three pictures, titled, respectively: "in harness," "faced round," and "tamed," are self-explanatory. Pictures six, seven, and eight progressively carry beast and man into a state of "forgetfulness" (while with each progression the beast's color alters, becoming lighter all the time). By picture number eight ("all forgotten"), the beast is now all white, and the man is perfectly at his ease. Then, in picture nine ("the solitary moon"), the beast is nowhere to be seen, and the oxherd becomes "master of his time." Finally, picture number ten simply depicts an empty circle—for both man and beast have vanished into oblivion.

The ox is, of course, representative of the animal aspect of the self being subjected to Zen discipline; the oxherd is the mind, which must learn to control the beast. The gradual whitening of the ox and his final disappear-

---

* *Manual of Zen Buddhism in the Bible of the World*, ed. Robert O. Ballou (London: Kegan Paul, Trench Trubner & Co., Ltd., 1940) pp. 367–376.

ance signifies the process of spiritual purification that comes with Zen practice. The final disappearance of both beast and man, to leave an empty circle, represents the ultimate Zen ideal.

As a summing up of the Zen ideal as part of the self-transformational process, we offer the following quote from Paul Reps's *Zen Flesh, Zen Bones.**

> The great path has no gates
> Thousands of roads enter it.
> When one passes through this gateless gate
> He walks freely between heaven and earth.

It need not be over-emphasized here that, essentially, this statement reflects—albeit in the sometimes confusing, but customarily, enigmatic Zen way of putting things—the usual ambition of the person embarking upon any of the normally accepted magickal and/or spiritual paths.

---

* London: M. Paterson & Co., 1959.

5 ☯ In harmony with universal energy

There is a reality even prior to heaven and earth;
Indeed, it has no form, much less a name;
Eyes fail to see it;
It has no voice for ears to detect;
Absolutely quiet, and yet illuminating in a mysterious way,
It allows itself to be perceived only by the clear-eyed.

Dai-o Kokushi
On Zen

The great universe
Is itself the Way of ai-ki.

Morihei Ueshlba
(founder of aikido)

A wide world lies half-way 'twixt heaven and earth.

Li hi-an
Philosophy of Half-and-Half

Of all the martial arts of the Orient, *aikido* ("Way of funda-mental, or divine, harmony" or "Way of harmony with universal energy") and *shorinji kempo* ("Shaolin temple fist

Way") appear to be among the most esoterically provoca-
tive, both in their physical practice, and in the mental and
spiritual attitude apparently adopted by those who partic-
ipate in these two unusual combat traditions. As is the
case with certain weapons arts, such as *kyudo* or Zen
archery, neither places any great emphasis on who is to
become the ultimate winner or loser in any specific contest
or bout; in the truest forms of aikido and shorinji kempo,
any hint of competition is, in any event, specifically dis-
couraged. The whole reason for taking part in either discipline is centered solely on spiritual self-development.
Koichi Tohei, one of the accepted early masters of aikido,
sums up this recommended attitude in his *Aikido in Daily
Life*,* which is as much a philosophical or spiritual treatise
as an essential handbook for aikidoists:

> In the first place, aikido is a discipline designed to
> penetrate to the inner meaning of the principle of
> non-dissension. In matches, someone must win,
> and winning in itself implies a heart filled with
> fighting. If you strive with all your might to win, it
> is doubtless very fine for your sportsmanship, but
> with the burning desire to be victorious you may
> develop the psychology that any means is all right
> if it helps you to win. This attitude can do great
> harm to you as a person.

There are some variations on the aikido theme
taught in dojos that tend to ignore its original spiritual
core, resulting in the all-too-prevalent Western emphasis
on the destructive and/or competitive aspects of the
art. We will deal here only with the original concepts of

---

* Tokyo, Rikugei Publishing House, 1966, p. 163.

aikido, as propounded by Master Tohei and its founder, Ueshiba Morihei.

Supernatural claims

Because of the almost supernatural claims surrounding its performance, aikido was greeted with much skepticism when it was first introduced to the West in demonstrations offered by the Japanese Minoru Mochizuki, in France, in 1951; and Koichi Tohei, in San Jose, California, in 1953. By all accounts, the dazzling techniques presented by these two aikido practitioners certainly defied description in rational terms. In particular, if contemporary reports are valid, Tohei's feats in San Jose were spectacular in the extreme. Without even raising a sweat, this former economics graduate, who entered aikido after training in the older and much-respected discipline of judo, easily threw five trained and well-built American judo experts who attacked him simultaneously. Two strong men could not tip him off an unstable four-legged stool (only three legs could touch the ground at the same time) while he was sitting with both feet raised off the floor. He resisted all attempts, again by someone much bigger and stronger than himself, to bend his outstretched, but fully relaxed, arm. Tohei could also render a stronger opponent helpless with a wrist lock applied with one hand and was able to prevent three sturdy American policemen from pushing him over by holding them off with just the tip of his little finger.

Although a short man, the amazing Tohei was built like an ox, and there were claims that his astounding feats were the result of some sort of counter-leverage technique. However, if any such assertions about the source of Tohei's strength of resistance could be proved to be true, the performances put up by his frail 85-year-old master, Ueshiba Morihei, the founder of the art of modern aikido, remain forever an enigma of startling proportions.

Ueshiba's chalk circle

The tiny Master Ueshiba was at the time around 5 feet tall and weighed about 144 pounds. In a stunning display of dexterity and skill, the agile 85-year-old aikido expert evaded all attempts to grab hold of him by a large group of men, including five U.S. military policemen, six judo and karate black belt holders, plus a couple of Japanese swordsmen, armed with oak swords. In another demonstration, the old man once challenged six newspapermen to attack him simultaneously, while he was standing within a chalk circle drawn on the floor. Hardly moving from the spot, he sent all six flying in various directions, with his feet all the time firmly planted within the circle.

But perhaps Ueshiba's most amazing demonstration—involving the more mystical aspect of aikido—came when he once told an audience that he was able to reduce his own body-weight by two-thirds. To demonstrate his claim, he placed twenty porcelain cups filled with tea in a circle on the floor. Then, stepping up onto the rim of the first, the old man walked around the complete circle on the rim of the teacups, without spilling a single drop of tea. Nor did he break or crack a single one of the delicate china cups.

Legends about Ueshiba abound and it was claimed that he and his pupil Tohei could, with their bare hands, fend off arrows fired at them. They were also reputedly able to avoid pistol bullets fired at almost point-blank range.

When, as an octogenarian, Ueshiba Morihei performed such amazing demonstrations of almost supernatural skill, he was already no stranger to the seemingly impossible. As a "young" 50-year-old, he was once scheduled to hold a command performance of his art before the Japanese emperor. Prior to the great day, he was stricken with a severe stomach illness but, dehydrated and weakened by continuous vomiting, he refused his disciples' entreaties to cancel the exhibition. Using his great powers of mind over body, the aikidoist adept straightened up immediately as he came into the presence of the emperor. His number one pupil, fearing that his master was only functioning at a fraction of his normal strength, held back in his attack. The pupil ended up with a fractured arm as Ueshiba threw him to the floor with all of his accustomed skill and strength. It was said that Ueshiba's three disciples, who took part in the 40-minute performance for the emperor, were forced to spend a week in bed to recover, while their master showed no further ill effects.

For the record, Ueshiba is not the only Japanese martial arts octogenarian seen to overcome much younger opponents. Maintenance of such high skills in the martial arts at a great age is not exclusively reserved to aikidoists. As an example, in 1986, the famed swordsman, Chutaro Ogawa, then aged 82, was observed to easily handle young 20 and 30-year-old pupils, staggering them with the force of his blows. Founder of *wado-ryu* karate, Hidenori Otsuka is another example of a martial artist of great age, who sparred effectively with his trainees when well into his eighties. These *budoka,* or followers of the *budo* doctrine of longevity, firmly believe that, with careful self-maintenance of ki, or internal energy, it is possible to improve, and not weaken, with age.

Genesis of aikido

When he was 28, Ueshiba first trained under the martial arts expert Sokaku Takeda, to learn the techniques that were later to form the physical basis of aikido. Takeda came from a long line of masters of the traditional *daito aiki-jutsu*, which had been supposedly founded by a Prince Teijun during the ninth century, and handed down through the years by members of the Minamoto family. Leaving Takeda after seven years, Ueshiba became for a while a disciple of a religious leader, Wanisaburo Deguchi, founder of a Shinto sect called Omoto-kyo, who preached human love and goodness as a means to world harmony (hence the name, aikido). For four years, Ueshiba lived as a solitary hermit in a remote abode on the holy mountain at Ayabe, sharing communion of spirit with his spiritual master. The three rules propounded by Deguchi for getting closer to God were: observation of nature, in order to understand the body of God; observation of the workings of the universe, in order to understand the energy of God; and observation of living beings, in order to understand the soul of the one true, living God. Understanding of the nature of the vitality of the universe, of its vital energy, or ki, played an all-important part, both in the master's teaching and his disciple's training.

According to its founder, aikido is a martial art of unique character, in which an aikidoist is able, through the operation of the mystical faculty, to actually sense or predict the move of a potential attacker, prior to the actual event. Ueshiba claimed that his own first true enlightenment regarding the purpose and meaning of the martial arts came in 1924, in Mongolia, when he found that he was able to avoid bullets shot at him by bandits through intuitively controlled movements of his body; and again, in 1925, when he was attacked by a Japanese naval officer wielding an oak sword. He simply "knew" each time exactly where the officer would strike, and could thus avoid being hit.

Later, while taking a walk in a garden in order to cool down, he experienced the phenomena of being rooted to the spot, while the earth appeared to be shaking. A golden light then issued forth from the ground beneath him, and transformed his own body into a golden one. By his own account, during the time Ueshiba was thus transfixed, he became aware of the "mind of God," and learned that the true source of the martial arts is Divine Love.

Ki and nen

Aikido's spiritual and philosophical roots lie deep within traditional Japanese Shintoism, with its avid expression of joy in nature's harmonious rhythms. (Ueshiba's original dojo was built alongside a Shinto temple, at Iwama, about 100 miles north of Tokyo.) There are also certain elements of Zen Buddhism and Confucianism, and a full comprehension of the essential importance of the all-pervading life force, the ki, as expressed in a unification of spirit (ki), mind (shin) and body (tai) into a trinity of harmony, will, and purpose. In addition to the expression ki, Ueshiba frequently used the Japanese word "nen" when describing the essence of aikido (nen connotes concentration, one-thought-pointedness, but has no exact English equivalent). According to aikido teaching, the cultivation of nen is: "The one-pointed concentration of the spirit as it seeks union with the universal reality that brought us into life on earth" (per Ueshiba Morihei, as quoted in *The Spirit of Aikido* by Kisshomaru Ueshiba).* In order to be able to best utilize the power of ki through use of nen, it must be kept in mind that the left side of the body is "the basis of martial art," and the right side is "where the ki of the universe appears."

All of this emphasis on super-normal techniques certainly elevates aikido into the realms of "magickal" practice, when viewed in terms of accepted Western occult tradition. Moreover, most other martial arts systems stress the need for contests and tournaments, but in keeping with the mentioned principles, aikido remains a strictly non-competitive art. In the words of Ueshiba's son and spiritual heir, Kisshomaru Ueshiba:

> A great temptation lures people into combative sports—everyone wants to be a winner—but there is nothing more detrimental to budo (Way of martial arts), whose ultimate aim is to become free of self, attain no-self, and thus realize what is truly human.†

Aikido methods

Ueshiba taught that in true budo there is no enemy, only a striving to be at one with the universe. He told his pupils never to look into the eye of an opponent, or at his/her sword, so as not to be lured by them, and to pray incessantly that a proposed fight would not, in fact, take place at all. The physical aspect of aikido is based on the uncomplicated principle of free, circular movements, sim-

---

* Tokyo, 1990, p. 36.
† Ibid.

ilar in effect to some of the more practical ju-jutsu techniques. In aikido, however, there is none of the complicated set of pushes, pulls, trips, kicks, and punches found in ju-jutsu, judo, and karate. The method is simple and straightforward. After an initial sharp punch to the face or ribs, if considered necessary to disconcert the attacker, the defender turns his own arms and body to follow the direction of attack taken by his opponent, diverting it past himself, instead of meeting it head-on in the way, for instance, of the karate-ka. While swinging back smoothly in an "S" curve, in an opposite direction to that first taken, the aikidoist will use an opponent's attempt to recover his own equilibrium to flip him backwards. The fact that the initial blow to an opponent's body may be ineffective in terms of stopping an attack is not important. It is the speed of throw, accomplished in a single, smooth movement, that provides the essence of the physical aspect of aikido.

The idea is not to wait for an attack—the art is just not to be there when it arrives; and to help the attacker on his way, in the direction he was originally moving. The method is to forget the self, the mind, and the body; and to allow the spiritual flow of life to take over and create a perfectly harmonious and effective movement. The prime object of aikido is not even to learn to throw, but to learn to free the numerous psychic, psychological, and physiological obstacles common to the modern person. It can be called the art of opening up the spirit.

Essential to all aikido practice is the use of correct breathing methods, with the ultimate aim of unifying body and soul through (as Koichi Tohei puts it) using "a breathing method that transcends breathing." The art is to forget one's own breathing while entering into a oneness with the universal. This is achieved on the practical level by aikidoists by sinking the spirit or consciousness, through mental imagery, into the hara, the single energy spot in the lower abdomen. Mental imagery is, in fact, constantly used in order to reprogram the subconscious to include only positive material.

Diversions from the original

Notwithstanding his old master's strict injunction against competitive aikido in any form, Kenji Tomiki, the first of Ueshiba's students to achieve an 8th dan status, has developed one of the better known of some 30 aikido styles that have come out of its founder's original teachings. Tomiki also studied judo under the legendary master Jigoro Kano, and his active, freestyle form of aikido places emphasis on tournament fighting. Ueshiba himself scorned free-form sparring as logically unacceptable. As originator of the aikido martial arts system, he was at all times firm in his conviction that aikido was an entirely defensive art, emphasizing the sophistication of mind and spirit within the student.

Although breaking away to form his own system, another of Ueshiba's disciples, Gozo Shioda, remained more spiritually faithful to his teacher, and he and Ueshiba always maintained a close relationship until the founder's death. Shioda was a top student of Ueshiba for 20 years, until he opened his own dojo. He was later recruited by the Tokyo police academy to teach aikido as an actual combat form to police recruits, and today he has more than 200 black belt instructors teaching his yoshinkan aikido to police personnel throughout Japan.

Aikido wrist locks are highly effective.

Shaolin temple fist way

In many ways, aikido is very close in character to the original ancient Chinese disciplines, which teach the need for a strict balancing of body, mind, and spirit—as witnessed at the first Shaolin temple. This places it in contrast to those Japanese martial arts that follow the original home-grown tradition of budo, the code of the samurai. There also remain, however, in aikido's spiritual content, many exclusively Japanese Shinto influences. On the other hand, the charismatic Doshin So's shorinji kempo was, from the start, directly influenced by the strictly Chinese tradition; its very name declaring its roots: "Shaolin temple fist way." Moreover, the Chinese word shaolin and the Japanese shorinji each translate as "young forest," clearly linking shorinji kempo to the Chinese Taoist "moving with the wind" principle so central to our current proposition, which includes correctly executed movement as a factor in stimulating contact with the inner self.

The founder of shorinji kempo was born Michiomi Nakano in Japan, in 1911, but raised by his grandfather in Manchuria. Under the patronage of a family friend, Mitsura Toyama, founder of the covert political organization known as the Black Dragon, Michiomi was, for 20 years, a member of various Japanese secret societies. At the time, he also acted as an agent for the Japanese secret service, and, as a cover, he became the disciple of a Taoist monk, Chin Ryo. Chin Ryo, in his turn, had secret links with a society known as Zaijari, an offshoot of the dreaded Chinese Triad movement. He also happened to be a master of a style of Shaolin temple boxing. Traveling around China with Chin Ryo, the young Japanese, Michiomi Nakano, studied a multitude of Chinese fighting techniques. He then contracted typhus, was persuaded to return to Japan, and, while a member of the Japanese Air Force, suffered a heart attack and was given one year to live.

Determined not to give in, Michiomi returned to his master, Chin Ryo, in Manchuria. Chin Ryo began to treat him with traditional forms of medicine, including acupuncture and massage. When the pair went to Peking in 1932, Michiomi was fit enough to join a Shaolin school, the Giwamonken, run by the master Bunta So. Michiomi took on the new name Doshin So, and just four years later was himself created 21st master of the northern Shaolin system Giwamonken school.

Pilgrimage to Shaolin

Doshin So now made a pilgrimage to the original Shaolin temple in northern China. There he was enthralled by the murals of martial arts figures which depicted a scene of friendly competition between Chinese and Indian monks. He realized that, for him, the future way was the way of peace. He became a great humanitarian and was deeply shocked by the disdainful way in which the Japanese military treated their own civilians when they retreated from the Chinese mainland at the start of World War II. Doshin So realized that there was a gap in the Japanese education system that did not allow for the teaching of compassion between various classes, or castes, of the race. In an interview on Japanese television, shortly before his death in 1981, he revealed that his prime reason for the creation of shorinji kempo was "to create a better relationship between Japanese people."

Returning from China in 1946, after World War II, to a defeated and demoralized Japan, Doshin So studied various Japanese martial arts forms, and even took up Western boxing for a period. But the Shaolin influence remained strongest within his soul. Shocked by the influence of black market gangsters, the yakuza, over post-war life in Japan, he founded a small group of young street fighters to combat the thugs. In a short while, Doshin So and his group cleaned up a small port town called Tadotsu, on Shikoku Island.

By now 40 years old, the dedicated, Chinese-trained martial arts master set up, at Tadotsu, the headquarters of his new school, based on his vision of how the original Shaolin monks conducted their lives. His Nihon Shorinji Kempo dojo became as much a temple at which to study Buddhism as a place to practice fighting arts, and was actually registered as a religion that followed the Kong Zen sect of Buddhism, and not as a form of martial art. As a religious organization, it has benefited from tax allocations, and today exerts a powerful influence over its more than one million members.

The shorinji kempo temple school, which has more than 800 training halls, is now headed by Doshin So's daughter, and is run as a religious, academic, and martial arts institution. The martial arts side of its education is closely linked with the Shaolin tradition of combat skills, combined with Zen Buddhist philosophical and religious principles. Shorinji kempo exponents who reach the rank of 3rd dan and above are expected to wear priest's robes denoting their rank.

Kongo Zen—the shared experience

During his lifetime, Doshin So was convinced that the Japanese form of Buddhism and the original fighting art had become corrupt. He strived throughout his life for a return to the first principles in each of the two disciplines, the metaphysical and the physical. He believed that modern Japanese-style Buddhism had become an empty ritualistic shell in which personal effort was no longer a prime consideration. His way was to return to the Indian interpretation of the Buddha's teaching, embracing the concept of the attainment of perfection in this lifetime, as opposed to a falling back on the doctrine of reincarnation, frequently used as an excuse for a person's shortcomings.

Doshin So promoted the concept that the intention behind physical training for the martial arts is not merely to knock one's opponent down, but is contained within the shared experience, the so-called Kongo Zen, enjoyed by pairs of sparring partners. The basic essence of Kongo Zen is related to the discovery within any individual of the natural laws that establish suitable ethical and moral laws. Students are encouraged to practice regularly with the same partner, so as to create an empathetic sense of cooperation, and to thus aid each other to reach a higher standard of proficiency.

The actual shorinji kempo technique, although firmly based on Shaolin temple boxing principles, contains elements of aikido and judo, and is visually as Japanese as either of the two mentioned martial arts. As seen in the aikido and judo systems, the prime accent in shorinji kempo is on defense; attack is used only as a last resort. The attack techniques center on the application of pressure to any one of 142 designated vital points on the body, to inflict either severe pain or—if considered necessary—actual physical damage. During training, shorinji kempo students are expected to experience pain through the use of this technique, and thus raise their own individual pain threshold.

As an adjunct to the religious and fighting arts training within the shorinji kempo syllabus, a form of traditional Japanese medicine known as *seiho* is taught. The practice of seiho embraces a style of acupuncture without needles, similar in concept to shiatsu, and a rejuvenation method based on stimulation of the nervous system and blood circulation, and of the alleviation of bone stress.

Philosophy of half and half

When shorinji kempo was first introduced to the West, its symbol created some controversy, due to ignorance of its ancient origins. The badge worn by shorinji kempo adherents is the *manji* symbol found on the walls of ruined temples throughout the world. The manji represents the cyclic progression of the cosmos and consists of two forms signifying the unity of opposites—one illustrating power, and the other, love. In a corrupted, inverted form it was used in Germany by the Nazis.

Principally, Doshin So's shorinji kempo, as is the case with Ueshiba's aikido, is prompted by very elevated moral principles. This tends to also raise it (again, as with aikido) beyond the general level of martial arts training as practiced, for instance, in China, where it is now a state-run activity with strictly no religious emphasis—and in much of Japan and the Western World, where there is sometimes less emphasis on morality and spirituality, and more on proficiency as a fighter.

The true essence of shorinji kempo is well illustrated by Doshin So's most oft-quoted saying: "Live half for

The shorinji kempo meditation posture known as zazen.

yourself and half for others." This statement reflects the deep Chinese influence over the founder of shorinji kempo practice and philosophy. It also echoes the teachings of the famous Tses-se, grandson of K'ung Fu-tse (Confucius), and the principles illustrated in the celebrated Chinese "Half-and-Half" song written by the poet Li Mi-an. This famous poem is included in the Chinese philosopher Lin Yutang's worldwide best-selling book on Chinese philosophy, *The Importance of Living*.* A key phrase in Li Mi-an's song, as translated by Lin Yutang, runs as follows:

> One half myself to Father Heaven I
> Return; the other half to children leave—
> Half thinking how for my posterity
> To plan and provide, and yet half minding how
> To answer God when the body's laid at rest.

This extract from an ancient poem is well in harmony with the spiritually-based philosophy residing behind both Ueshiba's aikido and Doshin So's shorinji kempo, which remain, perhaps, the most spiritual and/or magickal of the martial arts.

---

* London: William Heinemann Ltd., 1938, pp. 122 and 123.

6 ☯ Ways of the gods

If one man conquer in battle a thousand men, and if another conquer himself, he is the greatest of conquerors.

Anonymous Buddhist saying

Should anyone ask about the
spirit of Yamato (Japan)
It is the wild cherry blossom
Flowering
In the rising sun.

Norinaga

The myths of Japan relate that the eight islands that now make up Japan were created when the celestial pair Izanagi-na-mikoto and Izanami-na-mikoto "he-who-invites" and "she-who-invites"—were told to come down from heaven on a rainbow bridge, carrying with them a gift from the gods." This was a jewel-encrusted spear, a mystical phallic symbol, which Izanagi dipped into the then still primeval, oily ocean. The drops that fell from its tip congealed to form the eight islands of Japan. This scenario is central to the traditional Japanese belief system known as Shinto—literally "Way of the Gods."

According to Shinto philosophy, every natural thing—the wind, the sea, a river, a field, a tree, a mountain, a flower, an animal, or a human being possesses an invisible spirit. Furthermore, some parts of our physical world emanate from, or are descendants of, celestial deities. The spirits that inhabit the various aspects of our environment are specifically referred to as *kami* literally translated "highly placed beings." These are to be venerated, not totally as superhuman, but as divine and close to our world and daily life. The whole pantheon consists of a rich variety of hundreds of individual divinities representing a curious mix of Shinto and Buddhist, with some of dual parentage.

The Shinto connection

As much as Taoism, Confucianism, and Buddhism have been the principle sustaining forces behind the martial arts forms generated in China, so too has Japan's oldest indigenous religion, Shinto, played its part in shaping the nature of the martial arts in that country. When Buddhism was first introduced to Japan from China, there was an initial clash with the already-existing Shinto tradition, but harmony (and synthesis) eventually prevailed, in the typically pragmatic Japanese manner. The new Buddhist deities were perceived as a concrete manifestation of the previously invisible Shinto kami, and Shinto and Buddhist deities came to reside happily, side by side. Indeed, mainstream Buddhism in Japan is of the Mahayana ("greater vehicle") variety, a broad and varied system originating from China, and much influenced by Chinese folk religion, semi-mystical Taoism, and Confucianist social ethics.

For a time, the so-called Shugendo Buddhism was also very popular in Japan, a religion of magic, ritual, and enchantment that was formally banned during the Meiji era (1868–1912) and separated from Shinto in an effort to purify Japan's indigenous belief system.

It has been suggested, however, that the influence of Shinto and Buddhism upon each other has been very beneficial to Japanese society. The aesthetic/naturistic Shinto influence has, for instance, softened many of the sometimes harsh and grotesque features of Buddhist doctrine, art, and iconography, while Buddhism has offered a metaphysical understanding of death previously absent from Shinto thought. Most Japanese people who today profess other faiths such as Buddhism, Christianity, or Islam, and even atheists, still pay some homage to the ancient Shinto practices. Shinto is, to the Japanese, a religion beyond all other religions, having existed from the beginning of time, and not having been started by a specific individual, as have other faiths. Shinto represents an unbroken family link from one generation to another, starting with the first people, who were the biological progeny of the gods, or more correctly, the kami, which, in translation, simply means "that which is above."

Shinto ritual and sumo

Although it does not demonstrate too many of the fluid movements found in most other martial arts forms, of the Japanese fighting forms most firmly rooted in the old Shinto tradition, the most publicly prominent is *Sumo* wrestling. Moreover, throughout any sumo contest, and even during the preliminary buildup to a fight, the most prominent feature is the high visibility of Shinto magick-al practice.

In particular, at any sumo contest, there is a ceremonial purification of the fighting ring through sprinkling of salt and the placing of burnt offerings to the kami in the center of the ring. The sprinkling of salt is universal to all Japanese Shinto and Buddhist practice—for instance, salt is always sprinkled at and after funerals (in order to purify the home from the polluting influence of death). The use of salt as a good luck or purification symbol so strongly influences Japanese thought that priests have been known to come onto the field at major sporting events, such as baseball finals, to sprinkle salt, and improve team morale when their side looks to be in trouble.

Another specifically Shinto-influenced ceremony is the initiation rite called *dezuiri*, undergone by each newly promoted *yokozuna*, or grand champion, usually at a selected Shinto shrine. This consists of a noisy foot-stamping and hand-clapping dance that parallels the noise made by the kami in the mythical tale of the Sun Goddess, Amaterasu-o-mi-kami, one of whose direct descendants, Jinmu-tenno, became the first Emperor of Japan. The story goes that the glorious Amaterasu retreated in anger into a cave following wild behavior by her brother, Su-sa-no-wo, god of storm and tempest (and of love), who wreaked havoc by breaking down fences between rice fields and filling in irrigation ditches. With the world thrust into darkness, and in order to entice Amaterasu out of her cave, it is said that the remaining kami tried to lure her out by making noises.

Sumo wrestling is, indeed, steeped in folklore and magickal ritual. The old Japanese gods were reputed to have taken part in bare-handed battles and it was

A sumo wrestler sprinkling salt as a purification ritual.

customary for the early Japanese to settle disputes in hand-to-hand combat. It is recorded that, during the ninth century, the two sons of Emperor Buntoku even wrestled to decide who would take over their father's kingdom. An even earlier legendary contest—claimed to have taken place in the year 23 B.C.E.—has become deeply enshrined within sumo mythology, and is celebrated on July 7 each year, with a huge sumo event. The story centers on an enormous giant of a man named Kuyehaya, who was a great braggart and who considered himself the most powerful man in the world. The emperor of the day called for someone to challenge Kuyehaya, and a man named Sakune offered to fight the giant braggart. A wondrous duel commenced. The match started with Kuyehaya kicking Sakune in the ribs and breaking them. Undaunted, the plucky Sakune countered with a massive kick to Kuyehaya's groin which killed the giant in what has become enshrined as the first true sumo contest—the victorious Sakune remaining to this day the patron saint of Japanese sumo wrestling.

Early sumo wrestlers usually fought to the death, trampling their opponents after throwing them to the ground, but by the seventeenth century, sumo wrestling, or *kanjin-sumo,* had received official sanction as a martial art with its own codified set of rules and regulations. By the nineteenth century, sumo had become regarded as Japan's national sport, enjoying an enormous following, and with the hefty sumo wrestlers being treated almost like deities.

Formality and etiquette

Huge crowds gather to witness the giant sumo wrestlers competing in a *basho,* or sumo tournament, which takes place on the *dohyo,* a sand-covered dirt mound 15 feet in diameter. The participants, the *sumotori,* are always enormously heavy men who frequently tip the scales at around 300 pounds or more. Sumotori are, however, surprisingly light on their feet and exceedingly fit and healthy, with supple limbs and muscles. A special diet and exercise regime aids them in concentrating the major bulk of their weight into the lower portion of the body.

Tree-trunk legs, heavy hips, and a large protruding stomach also help create the low center of gravity needed to remain on their feet—for the contest ends immediately once any part of the body above the knee touches or lands on the surface of the dohyo. The fight is also over if any part of the body touches the ground outside the contest area. When a contestant is declared a winner, no protest is allowed and the referee's decision is always accepted as final. The match can be over in a few seconds and rarely goes on for more than a minute.

The 48 classical moves of the sumotori include variations involving throwing, pushing, tripping, and pulling. One of the most spectacular of the techniques used is the *hataki-komi.* Sensing that his opponent is coming in for a final effort, the sumo wrestler steps deftly aside and slaps his opposite number on the back to carry him out of the ring on his own power.

An enormous amount of formality and etiquette surrounds the practice of sumo. The contest commences with a lengthy Shinto ceremony—lasting over half an hour—and includes a line-up of sumotori dressed in specially embroidered ceremonial kimonos, or aprons—indicating their status as sumo wrestlers. For the fight, the sumo wrestler is clad in a *mawashi*, a single silk loincloth around 30 feet long and 2 feet wide. The mawashi is folded into four and wrapped around the sumotori like a baby's diaper.

Many sumo contests are held at Shinto shrines, where the first such events took place hundreds of years ago. A Shinto priest is always in attendance at a sumo bout and officiates in the compulsory salt-purifying ceremony performed by each of the contestants during the preliminary ceremony leading up to the bout. Before the fight begins, the sumotori will stamp their feet to drive all evil spirits from the ring. They will then face each other in various crouching positions for four minutes, in an attempt to stare each other down and thus gain some psychological advantage. The start of the bout proper, the *shobu*, is then signaled by the referee and, like two great bulls coming together to lock horns, the wrestlers will charge each other and meet in the center of the dohyo with a resounding crash. This initial charge is known as the *tachiai* and represents, for the sumo wrestler, a veritable moment of truth after years and months of rigid discipline and tough physical preparation.

Specifically, the main ritualistic actions made by the sumo wrestler during the *dohyo-iri* or ring-entering ceremony prior to combat include: clapping as a ritual to indicate the presence of one whose soul is pure; lifting the apron to drive out devils; and the raising of both arms to show the absence of concealed weapons (a legacy from samurai days). Flanked by two attendants (the *tsuyu harai* or "herald," and the *tachi mochi* or "sword bearer"), the sumo wrestler will then squat at the edge of the ring and produce two resounding claps, arms outstretched, in a symbolic purification of the grass on the field of battle. He then rises and moves to the northern end of the ring (to face the Emperor), and claps once more. Next, placing his left hand over his heart, and with his right arm pointing east, he raises his right leg and brings it crashing down onto the ground. This movement, repeated with the other leg and known as *shiko*, both frightens away evil spirits and heralds his intention to beat his opponent into the dust.

According to the unwritten code of the sumo art, a *yokozuna* (grand champion) must voluntarily retire if he fails to win eight bouts in a row. When he reaches the grade of the *maku-uchi*, the top-ranking sumo grade, he is permitted to wear his hair in the familiar top-knot style, marking him as a supreme performer. The dressing of a sumo wrestler's hair is done by a professional hairdresser from his own particular sumo stable. Only when he retires can it be cut in a special ritual, known as *danpatsu-shiki*, performed by his patrons and colleagues.

Samurai influence

A significant number of Japanese martial arts forms have developed out of, or been influenced by, a synthesis of traditional Shinto and Buddhist beliefs and the original combat skills of the famous Japanese samurai warriors. In 1876, the samurai were officially deprived of the right to carry arms. They proceeded to adapt an ancient fighting form called *ju-jutsu* to their needs. Ju-jutsu was a rough-and-tumble type of martial art that had already been practiced in Japan for some 2,000 years (see Chapter

7). However, as a direct result of samurai activity, an infinitely more refined and deadly martial arts system evolved, producing what might be termed the "ultimate warrior."

The wondrous arts of the ninja

For over 500 years the *bushi,* or samurai, in his traditional suit of armor that contained several thousand pieces, strode in all his glory through the pages of Japanese history. Throughout this period, the infinitely more secret, and very much misunderstood, *ninja* lived side by side with his more-visible counterpart. Because of the secret nature of ninja training, which remains to this day, little is known of the true motivation of this legendary warrior of the night. It is known, however, that, traditionally, the ninja was required to develop and sustain a wide range of what can only be termed psychic or magickal powers. These esoteric skills moved far beyond the more visible, everyday "dirty tricks" ninja accomplishments, such as the arts of disguise, of stealth, and of combat, both unarmed and armed with an array of weaponry, standard and improvised.

Ninja training offered not only a means of protection when attacked, but taught a variety of effective responses to any assault threat. *Tai-jutsu* body movements in *ninjutsu* are still based on the five-element theory—earth, air, fire, water, and space: the qualities of each element describe a possible type of body movement. Also taught were the virtues of physical fitness and endurance. Ninjas were known to be able to survive conditions in the most barren of terrains for weeks on end. Any ninja could run or swim for miles at a fast speed without becoming fatigued, climb walls and trees, walk across narrow gorges, and scale precipices. Sleeping in a tree without falling out was another unique ninja skill and, from an early age, instruction was given on how to dislocate limbs at will, in order to enter buildings through small apertures—or to effect a miraculous escape when tied up with chains or other bonds. The ninja was also schooled to, when necessary, kill with the utmost efficiency, and in a variety of stealthy ways.

Yoko aruki, or sideways walking, is another of the many amazing ninja skills. This is a means of walking whereby the user's footprints do not reveal the direction he or she is traveling and which enables him or her to walk in complete silence through town or country.

The list of almost magickal ninja arts continues: *Goton-no-jutsu*—or the five escaping techniques—teaches how to hide using trees or grass, walls and rocks, and even the bare ground—plus diversionary tactics involving the use of fire and metal objects, and escape methods by water that included learning how to hold the breath under water for extended periods; *horoshi-jutsu* was the name given to the art of using fire for a multitude of purposes, diversionary or otherwise; *shinso toho no-jutsu,* literally, "the way of the rabbit in the deep grass," refers to an exceptionally acrobatic technique that enabled a ninja to walk on his or her hands in the dark in order to avoid tripping over anything; *ten-mon* ("meteorology") was the art of recognizing the subtle signals in the environment in order to predict the weather.

As the most comprehensive of all the martial arts forms, traditional ninjutsu contains elements of all the other known combat forms, and has become the most total form of self-protection ever known, using both weapons of a large and dazzling variety, and unparalleled skill in unarmed combat forms. The ninja of old was able to creep in undetected from out of the night, make a kill, and disappear like a phantom. This proclivity for working in shadows and in the dark has resulted in the term "shadow warrior."

Ninjas were always expected to be highly intelligent individuals, adept in the arts of flattery, deception, and disguise. The art of disguise, or *shichi-ho-de* (literally, "seven ways of going"), was named for the seven major characters a male ninja was taught to impersonate: traveling actor, itinerant priest, mountain priest, Buddhist priest, fisherman, farmer, and merchant. Female ninjas, the *kuno-ichi*, would pose as delicate geisha girls, or shrine attendants, or disguise themselves as harmless serving girls or prostitutes to gain easy entry to a house. Being as proficient in the ways of the ninja as their male counterparts, they were sometimes even more feared. As ninjutsu is not based on power punching and kicking, but upon natural, flexible body movements, it is one of the few martial arts systems where women are seldom at some physical disadvantage.

When not in disguise, a ninja would generally don a costume called a *shinobi shozoku*, consisting of jacket, hood, and fitted pants that were tightly tied at the knee and ankle to allow for mobility of movement. This gear was generally reversible, red or black on one side, dark blue, green or white on the other. Footwear was lightweight in design and had a split at the toe to ensure better grip and silence in movement.

"I am the compassionate one; but he who always sees and knows with all senses"—the image of the ninja.

Spiritual roots

There remains some problem in trying to define exactly what a ninja was or is. Judging by available historical data, one can largely discount the almost wholly negative image presented to date in most fiction books and films. The majority of these presentations are based on slipshod or virtually non-existent historical research. The near "ninjamania" of the 1980s and into the 1990s is, unfortunately, primarily the product of the imaginations of novel and script writers—and of those persons who have set themselves up as teachers of a "lost art," without actually holding the credentials to do the job.

The fact is that the true ninja, as much as any of his counterparts in any of the other martial arts, comes from a tradition steeped in basically spiritual values—mainly of the Shinto variety, but with some Buddhist influence.

The aristocratic era of the samurai warrior culture dominated Japan for a considerable period of time. The first seeds of the still-to-come ninja were planted in the isolated wilderness of the Kii Peninsula by certain Chinese warriors, scholars, and monks fleeing repression by the samurai overlords. With them came the already ancient religious, philosophical, and cultural concepts of China and Tibet, such as the Buddhist tantra and other traditions. The original inhabitants of the Kii region, mountain warriors and priests, were steeped in early Japanese Shinto belief—the equivalent of the animistic beliefs of other aboriginal peoples around the world—and also had rudimentary knowledge of such subjects as astrology, cane and staff fighting, and, more importantly, *kaijutsu*, a Taoistic type of ability to live in harmony with the universe. These ancient Japanese warrior-priests, who were already well conversant with many magickal practices, quickly absorbed all they could learn from their new Chinese neighbors, to create an integrated synthesis that would provide the basis for later ninja training.

Occult connections

Another historical factor behind the origin of the ninja was the religious struggle that occurred between the followers of Buddhism and the followers of the traditional Japanese religion, Shintoism. During a period of bitter acrimony between the two doctrines, the Shugendo Buddhists, in particular (a movement rooted in the ancient Japanese worship of mountains as supernatural realms for the gods), were forced to flee to mountain strongholds in the remote areas of Iga and Koga on Japan's main island of Honshu. For 400 years these mountain warrior priests, the *yamabushi*, zealously guarded the secrets of the arts of the ninja, which they had developed through long periods of meditation and through study of some of the more occult-based Shugendo Buddhist teachings.

In ninja esoteric practice there is also a strong motivating element based on the Mikkyo Buddhism of the *Shingon* tradition, notable for its emphasis on *mudra* (special positions of the hands), *mandala* (visualization and meditation on sacred circular forms) and *mantra* (sacred vocalization), and on the use of fire in its rituals. Further back, in its Tibetan/Chinese origins, Shingon is related to the various forms of tantric yoga, having come to Japan directly out of the Chinese Chen Yen ("True Word") tantric sect. One important aspect of the Shingon tradition that connects with the ninja perspective is the emphasis placed on secrecy with regard to transmission of occult knowledge. Other than the passing on of certain key mantras and so on by word of mouth, from master to pupil, Shingon secrets are usually portrayed symbolically only in sacred art.

Yet another important group of individuals to influence early ninja development were the so-called *sennon* mountain recluses, who worked directly with natural laws and were thought to have supernatural powers. These Japanese shamans worked in concert with animal spirits, much like the native North American Indian and other shaman-directed cultures.

According to Dr. Masaki Hatsumi, in his book, *The Realm of the Ninja*,* the ninja emerged as a counter-culture response to the ruling samurai elite, being forced to develop martial arts skills secretly, because no one other than the samurai were at the time permitted to carry arms or develop fighting skills. The shugendo priests, for instance, were stripped of the right to defend their land-holdings and were even further persecuted because the samurai overlords resented their freedom of spirit, exemplified in the fact that the shugenja considered every person a priest in his or her own right.

The ultimate goal of the early forerunners of the ninja (the mountain warrior priests and shamans) was spiritual enlightenment, as embodied in their practice of shugendo and other forms of warrior asceticism and power development. Ninjutsu thus became embued with esoteric and mystical influences from its inception. Within the confines of the true art of ninjutsu, as practiced

---

* Hollywood: Unique Publications, 1981.

today by the very few existing direct-line descendants of the ninjas of the past, this emphasis on spiritual development remains a key factor.

Dr. Hatsumi records that the ancestors of the ninja lived the lives of "naturalists and mystics."* In his present-day curriculum, the American ninja instructor, Stephen K. Hayes, stresses the need for a balance between the physical and mystical aspects of ninjutsu training: "It would be suicidal to become an expert in the skills of driving an automobile while ignoring the study of traffic signals and regulations."†

The ninja as magician

In his book *Mind of the Ninja: Exploring the Inner Power*,†† psychologist Kirtland C. Petersen provides a fascinating survey of the entire ninja ethos. In particular, he notes several archetypes of the ninja, both negative and positive, and past and present, that have been presented mainly in literature and on film. These include: the ninja, in negative mode, as the Shadow, Energy, Death, and rebirth, and even as Lucifer (whom Petersen, incorrectly, equates with the Devil); the ninja, in positive mode, as the Warrior and the Warrior's Quest, the Actor, the Healer or Shaman, the Alchemist, and the Magician. He also discusses ninja "archetypes of the spirit," such as the Hermit, and the Wise Old Man, which archetype he equates with the "superior insight" of the ninja. Of special interest in

---

* Ibid.

† *Ninjutsu.* (Chicago: Contemporary Books, 1984), p. 149.

†† Chicago: Contemporary Books, 1986.

our present study is Petersen's summary of the qualities that make up ninja/the Magician:

> The magician has many qualities. He symbolizes, among other things, the ability to harness the powers of nature consciously, and to put these energies to creative use. The Magician is also capable of fooling us with deception and illusion. But at the same time, and more positively, he is capable of showing us that what we so often take as "reality" is but "appearance." He is, therefore, able to take us through the illusory surface of things to the fundamental oneness beneath reality as we normally see it.*

If this definition fits the legendary shadow warrior, there can be no doubt that the traditional ninja practiced a form of magick, and that the so-called "modern ninja" probably still uses certain magickal routines, even if these are not acknowledged as such. One known magickal routine still used by ninja adepts is the art of *ketsu-in*, or employment of specified finger positions for the channeling of ch'i/ki energy—an operation similar to the hand mudras used by certain Tibetan Buddhists for the same reason, and to be equated with other known magickal techniques of other traditions. Specified sounds are associated with each hand position (see Chapter 10). The proper channeling of psychic or ki energy through this method can be used to block or cut off an opponent's energy field (as we have heard earlier), to balance the energy flow in the body, and even to promote healing.

Also in keeping with accepted magickal aims and practice, the development of the wholly intuitive

---

* Ibid., p. 234.

response was (and still is) a paramount aim in ninja training. Moreover, the early developers of ninjutsu held the belief that the very mountains in which they lived possessed a certain power, and that people were capable of achieving their own comparable personal power through a form of training that took the body beyond its normal limits of physical endurance. The method used to tame the forces of nature was simply to become totally immersed within these forces. Direct experience of the powers of nature and of the powers of the body was placed ahead of mere technique. This attitude reflected an especially deep understanding of the concept of ki/ch'i. Thus, the total immersion experience is considered an essential factor in the ninja's training into the art of taijutsu, or empty-handed combat. It is a case of moving from mere knowledge of any technique or form, to *becoming* that technique or form.

Comparisons with other "Old Religions"

Both the Shinto religion and the practice of ninjutsu are similar in in many respects to the so-called "Old Religions" of our planet, such as, for instance, tantra and wicca. At their roots, all are fundamentally the same. Modern wicca, as practiced in the United States and elsewhere, is based on an ancient, pagan nature cult, with sensuous overtones that reflect connections with an instinctive folk wisdom that transcends in many ways our modern science and technology.

The earliest Shinto teachings provided a picture of a neutral world and universe that was, in its essence, neither friendly nor hostile, but subject to natural laws that could be used for either beneficent or harmful effects, depending on the quality and aptitude of the individual involved. This concept equates almost exactly with the beliefs of both modern and ancient witchcraft or wicca and those of the ancient Indian tantric system. All apparently have their origin in early fertility practices, with emphasis placed on the divine female power.

The theme relating to constructive use of sexual energies, within the context of the "Old Religions," will be further developed in Chapter 8, which deals with one of the more exotic Japanese martial arts offshoots that has its own roots deep within pagan fertility ritual. It is sufficient to emphasize here both the clear link that exists between the more ancient religious practices of all countries and continents, and the striving for harmony and balance on all levels, that typifies the religious (and martial arts) disciplines of the East.

7 ☯ From high kicks to empty hand

The wise and thoughtful man attacks his faults.

Zen Buddhist saying

My body is like a drifting cloud—
I ask for nothing. I want nothing.

Kamo No Chomei, *Hojoki*

Each of the Oriental countries has, at some time or another, influenced its neighbors in the development of a particular form or variation of the martial arts. Although the Chinese, Japanese, and Korean styles carry within themselves some recognizable national traits, there is a fine strand from a mutual spinning wheel threading its way through all of them. Any effort to trace the exact origins of a particular country's martial arts systems can lead to the way becoming increasingly unclear, the further one goes back into time.

Certain Oriental martial arts forms also lean more toward the physical than the mystical, but all contain some spiritual elements and are deserving of mention in our overall context.

Way of the foot and fist

At first glance, the high-kicking style seen in Korean *taek-won-do* looks so similar to the northern Chinese Shaolin temple methods that a distinct Chinese connection is suggested. There is evidence, however, that the Korean kicking style was in existence as long as 2,000 years ago, which means that it may have been the Koreans who influenced the Chinese, and not vice versa. The term taek-won-do means literally "way of the foot and fist." Legend implies that the first Korean martial arts style was created by a fifth century Buddhist monk named Won Kwang. The original art of taekwon-do was known as *tae-kyon* and flowered in the tiny Korean kingdom of Silla during the reign of King Chin Heung—who desperately required the services of a warrior elite to combat the warlike intentions of troublesome neighboring kingdoms, Baek Je and Koguryo. The king of Silla's warriors became known as the *hwrang-do,* literally "way of the flowering manhood," and based their philosophical and martial art practice on the five precepts put forward by the Buddhist monk Won Kwang. These were:

1. Be loyal to your king.
2. Be obedient to your parents.
3. Be honorable to your friends.
4. Never retreat in battle.
5. Make a just kill.

The hwrang-do always performed their marching and training at three times the normally accepted speed. This super-fit young fighting corps incorporated the use of unarmed combat forms to supplement their main weapons—the spear, the bow, the sword, and the hooked staff. The inner elect of the hwrang-do were known as the *sul-sa* and their martial arts feats were regarded as almost magickal. They were revered by their own people and feared by their enemies, and gained a measure of prestige comparable with that enjoyed by the legendary Japanese samurai warriors. Their great skill at unarmed combat also inspired the general populace of Silla to take up the practice of *tae-kyon*, which became something of a national sport.

The warriors of Silla used two major martial arts styles: the hand-method was named tae-kyon, and the foot-based form, *soo-bak*. Their enemies in Koguryo, to the

High-flying mid-air kicks are a spectacular feature of taekwon-do.

north, practiced a method called *soo bak-gi*, which contained spectacular flying kicks that were to become, in later years, the hallmark of typical Korean taekwon-do. When the strong Koryo dynasty took over affairs, there was an active encouragement of the practice of tae-kyon among the general populace. It was, indeed, compulsory for some 500 years for all young Korean men aged six and upward to train in the art.

After a Japanese-imposed ban on martial arts practice in Korea between 1909 and 1945, a Korean post-war army general, Choi Hong Hi, was instrumental in initiating a modern revival among his countrymen. Choi was a determined character who, as a 12-year-old boy, was expelled from school for daring to criticize the then-ruling Japanese. Eventually imprisoned by the Japanese military authorities, he taught the Korean martial art to both his cell-mate and his jailer. After his release by the Japanese, Choi became a leading light in a Korean students' resistance movement, was re-arrested, and sentenced to death. Only the end of the war soon afterward, in 1945, saved his life.

Somewhere along the line, he had picked up a karate black belt to add to his tae-kyon expertise, and soon developed his own style, which he initially called *chang hun*. He was later instrumental, during the 1950s, in having the name taekwon-do accepted as the title of the distinctive Korean form of the martial arts. Taekwon-do has since become the official national sport of Korea.

During the 1960s, General Choi got caught up again with political problems and was forced to leave Korea. The Korean government immediately set up the rival World Taekwon-do Federation, in an effort to replace the Choi-dominated International Taekwon-do Federation.

Taekwon-do has since become the official national sport of Korea. General Choi's influence on taekwon-do remains world-wide and his monumental 15-volume encyclopedia of the art contains no fewer than 3,200 techniques. His teaching is based on five principles similar to those given by Wong Kang 1,400 years before him; namely: integrity, courtesy, perseverance, self-control, and indomitable spirit.

The special feature of taekwon-do is its high-flying kicks of enormous destructive power—although its basic technique is one of self-defense. The aim of a taekwon-do practitioner is to dispatch an opponent with a single deadly blow to any one of 69 vital spots, or *kup so*, located on the body. The number of spectacular mid-air and other kicks make it a favorite spectator contest. A taekwon-do expert can launch himself up to 10 feet into the air, and deliver a whole series of kicks before he again touches the ground. Flexibility of back and legs are a prerequisite in a tough training schedule. Emphasis is also placed on the theory of attainment of a high degree of physical power, called by General Choi, *him ui wolli*. Force is amplified by such techniques as pulling one fist back to the hip while the other is throwing a punch to counter an opponent's charge. As in the karate kiai technique, a sharp exhalation of breath at the moment of impact assists in focusing power into an attack. To prevent serious injury during competition or training, taekwon-do participants wear a variety of body-armor padding on chest, hands, and instep so that full-contact blows and kicks can be executed. The taekwon-do training hall is known as a *dojon* and there is a similar color grading and dan degree system to that found in karate and judo.

Other Korean martial arts forms similar to taek-won-do include the disarmingly devastating *hapkido* and *kuk sool won,* which has gained some popularity in the United States.

The quality of running water

In contrast to the aggressive-from-the-start taekwon-do, the hapkido technique calls for an initial gentle response, similar to that used in judo and aikido. But once an opponent has been thrown off balance by a soft, circular, yielding block, the hapkidoist swings into action with an assortment of kicks and blows that are even more devastating than those encountered in karate and taekwon-do. Hapkido offers many choices in reply to an attack, flows smoothly and, with its success dependent more on skill than strength, is an awesome self-defense weapon.

Hapkido means "the art of coordinated power." It works on the principle that felling an attacker is not enough. The object is to make a first strike so effective that an assailant will never be able to get up for a counterattack. This places hapkido outside the parameters of a sporting contest and it is used solely as a stunningly effective means of self-defense. Response by a Hapkido expert to an attack is usually instinctive, and deadly, and it would be well-nigh impossible for a hapkidoist to tone down his technique to suit competition requirements.

Hapkido's history dates from the days of the Buddhist monks of the fifth century, and was revived as a modern martial art by a Korean named Yong Sul Choi. Yong Sul based his style primarily on the principle of the motion of water running downhill, and the way in which it parts to flow around an obstacle in its path. This quality of water is regarded as the foundation on which hapkido rests and the concept correlates with the chi phenomena in Chinese k'ung-fu and the ki flow in Japanese karate. Yong Sul Choi lived for 40 years in Japan, where he absorbed the skills of the old aiki-jutsu and of ju-jutsu. He introduced his hapkido to Korea after World War II. One of his students, Bong Soo Han, has since settled in the United States and introduced hapkido to the West.

The fighting style known as kuk sool won places stress on physical fitness and includes in its program a variety of falling techniques, joint locks, kicks, and breaking feats similar to those displayed by certain k'ung-fu and karate experts. An extension of the kuk sool won style involves the deft use of an ordinary walking stick or cane as an effective self-defense weapon. It has been claimed that the martial art of kuk sool won dates back over a thousand years. Its leading exponent in the United States is an expatriate Korean, Dr. He Yung Kim, who has practiced the art for over 35 years.

More mystical arts of Korea

In the present context, one of the more interesting of Korean styles is the rather mystical *tang soo do*. Regarded by its adherents as something of a spiritual path, tang soo do exhibits some possibilities of Chinese cross influence, while some observers have also likened it to the Japanese shotokan karate style, with the addition of taekwon-do-type high kicks. The objective of a tang soo do student is to subtly balance the physical and the metaphysical aspects of his personality. Its name, "way of the knife hand," is something of a misnomer. As is the case with most of the Korean fighting disciplines, it centers its main form of attack around spectacular high-kicking. Moreover, tang soo do techniques and routines are clearly linked with the older and more esoteric *sul sa do* fighting traditions.

Of special interest to note is that a breakdown of the term "sul sa do" provides the following information: sul = "magick"; sa = "personal secret"; do = "art" or "way"— i.e., this very ancient martial arts form is clearly linked with concepts of secret magickal knowledge and rites. Historically, sul sa do emerged around the fifth century from the regions controlled by the Koguryo dynasty, one of the sworn enemies of the kingdom of Silla, mentioned above. Both weaponry and empty-handed skills, plus the arts of dance, literature, science (magic), archery, and charioteering were on the curriculum, making the Koguryo warriors magicians, scholars, and fighters.

Sul sa do (also known as *moo sul*), which incorporates aspects of the even more ancient *soo bahk do,* survived the centuries of strife and turmoil that have marked Korea's history, being revitalized from time to time by specific masters of the art. In 1945, an institution named Moo Duk Kwan—Institute of Martial Virtue—was established by master Hwang Kee, who as a young man learned martial arts techniques in China. Hwang Kee's techniques were also firmly based in soo bahk do and sul sa do, and it was he who coined the new term, tang soo do. Like hapkido and kuk sool won, the art of tang soo do has become popular in the United States, and worldwide boasts some 20,000 black belt holders. In 1981, its founder paid a visit to the United States, where he was highly impressed with the progress made in the teaching of his unique taekwon-do style in that country. Hwang Kee has also authored a highly definitive historical and training manual about tang soo do.

Technique of flexibility

In 1876, when the famed samurai warriors were officially deprived of the right to carry arms, it became imperative to develop some system of fighting without weapons. Ju-jutsu, which can be termed a rough-and-tumble type of martial art, had already been practiced in Japan for some 2,000 years, but, by the normal Oriental martial arts standards, it is a rather basic and unphilosophical system. Its original function was simply to disarm an opponent before going in for the kill, and it should certainly not be confused with the much gentler and sporting art of judo—which has become so popular in the west and is a regular feature at the Olympic Games.

Although the Japanese word *ju* can be translated as submission, and the expression ju-jutsu means "the technique of flexibility," there is nothing soft or gentle about the ancient martial art that was first used by Japan's legendary samurai warriors for unarmed combat purposes. Traditionally, when facing up to bandits or *ronin*—lawless members of his own calling—a samurai would only resort to unarmed combat if he could not get his sword out in time, or was somehow dispossessed of his weapon. Nor did he find it that easy to perform grapples, holds, and throws, burdened as he normally was by a heavy suit of traditional armor.

The original ju-jutsu comprises the use of a series of throws, holds, and locks that are carried out in such a way that the application of additional pressure may result in the actual dislocation of a joint or the breaking of a bone. There are also various kicks and punches similar to those used in karate.

The samurai version of ju-jutsu was codified during the sixteenth century by Hisamori Takenouchi, and included the use of a variety of weapons, including the *naginata*, a curved-bladed spear with a three-foot long blade, and a shaft of a little over four feet. This became the favorite weapon of the bushi women, the wives of the bushido (samurai) warrior class. The slightly lighter and straight *yari* spear eventually replaced the naginata in a samurai's armory. Another major ju-jutsu weapon of the samurai, other than his perennial sword, was the wooden *bo* staff.

The practice of ju-jutsu itself is, above all else and in its original form, essentially a warrior's martial art that provides a quick and effective method of neutralizing an opponent. As such, it is an excellent method of self-defense against muggers, and has also been used extensively as a basic training skill among wartime commandos and secret service units around the world. Ju-jutsu has, in recent generations, become classified as a sport but has, by necessity, had many of its lethal techniques deleted from use. Traditionally minded exponents stolidly refuse to accept this watering down of their deadly art, and refrain from taking part in any sort of competition. Some of its more esoteric practices relating to healing are covered in Chapter 10.

The yielding way

A student of ju-jutsu during the late nineteenth century is acknowledged as the "father" of the widely practiced sport called judo. The word judo means "the gentle way," and its founder, Dr. Jigoro Kano, created this new sporting form in order to place emphasis more on the moral, intellectual, and physical training aspects of the martial arts—as opposed to the purely combative. There is also, in judo, a lack of the more intense mysticism found in some of the other, older martial arts systems.

As a rather sickly child, Kano studied ju-jutsu in order to build up his health and, in the process, discovered the inner ethical core of the samurai warrior tradition. He was also influenced by the philosophy contained within the teachings of soft-school Chinese martial arts like t'ai chi. As a graduate in literature and politics at Tokyo University, he spoke and read English fluently and was well versed in the philosophies of his own and other countries. By 1882, when he was still only 22, Kano had founded his own style, initially called *kano-ryu* but later renamed *kodokan judo*. He worked on the principles of maximum effect with minimum effort, and trained his students to always maintain a genuine respect for their opponents.

While still running his own school of judo, Kano became a master of the *kito-ryu* and *tenshinshiyo-ryu* ju-jutsu systems, and fought and defeated the ju-jutsu champion of the time. When his judo school easily won a competition arranged against various ju-jutsu schools, his new form of martial arts swiftly gained recognition. Kano's pioneering form of judo was greatly modified in later years, especially after it became an exciting and invigorating Western sport of some proportion. Because of an anti-boxing movement at the time, it gained particular momentum in the United Kingdom, from 1948 onward, when the British Judo Association was formed. By 1952, the International Judo Federation had been inaugurated, and, by the early 1960s, judo had become a subject at many schools in its 70 member-nations. Finally, in 1964, judo, as a major competitive sport, was introduced at the Tokyo Olympics. Dr. Jigoro Kano, the "father" of judo, was also founder of the Japanese Olympic Committee, and died at sea, in 1938, on his way home from the Cairo International Olympic Conference.

Strict discipline

The judo exponent, or judo-ka, wears a white, kimono-style top and trousers (*judogi*), similar to that used in karate and other martial arts forms, but with a special, heavy cotton jacket that will not tear easily when grabbed. As in karate and other disciplines, a strict etiquette is observed in the judo dojo.

Also following the example of karate, the central pillar of the judo discipline is the practice of *katas,* the forms or movements used in training. Sparring is known as *randori,* literally "free sparring."

Although there are many subdivisions contained within the curriculum of the judo system, there are four basic categories of technique: standing techniques, (*tachiwaza*); throwing techniques (*nagewaza*); and ground techniques (*newaza*); a fourth technique, *atemiwaza,* is similar to the ju-jutsu pressure point striking method and is only taught for self-defense, and is banned from competitive use.

The standing techniques involve a system of blocking movements to avoid being thrown. The various throws are used in order to get an opponent onto the ground, so that holding techniques can be employed in order to gain control without causing injury. The choking techniques referred to previously involve methods of obstructing either the breath or the flow of blood to the brain.

Strength plays little part in the contest and the art of judo lies more in the ability to predict the move an opponent will make, and then to effect timely application of the power of resistance, in perfect coordination with the act of yielding.

As in karate, there is a grading and belt system in judo, known as ranking. Also as in karate, 9th and 10th dans wear belts that signify their completion of a full cycle. As the only 12th dan in judo history, Jogoro Kano, founder of the art, wore a white belt to show that he had transcended all methods of ranking.

Art of the empty hand

Like stepping stones in a stream, the scattered chain of the Ryukyu Islands links the main islands of Japan to the Chinese offshore island of Taiwan, or Formosa as it was originally known. The largest of the Ryukyu islands is Okinawa, 340 miles due east of China, and about 6 miles wide and 70 miles long. Most of its inhabitants came originally from the South Asia mainland. Some Japanese warriors also settled in Okinawa after fleeing there during a war in their own country. The introduction from Japan of Buddhism during the thirteenth century brought a further increase in Japanese influence. At the time the Japanese first realized the strategic importance of Okinawa, placed as it was on the sea route to China, the unsophisticated Okinawans, many of whom were of Chinese descent, lived mainly as farmers and fisherman. In 1609, the Japanese ruler, the Tokugawa Shogun, encouraged an invasion of Okinawa by the militant Satsuma clan—although Okinawa remained technically under Chinese rule and continued to pay a biennial tribute to China right up until 1871. In the intervening years, this small island was also to be the essential link between Chinese and other Asian mainland martial arts forms, and those already developed in Japan.

When the Chinese forms of combat were first introduced to Japan via Okinawa, there was already in that country a long tradition of martial-type arts involving the use of a variety of weapons, from the bow to the sword. The Japanese lived according to a strict code of rules. The philosophy which lies at the heart of each of the major martial arts of the world was already deeply imbued within the consciousness of the renowned Japanese samurai warriors, and of the mysterious and much-feared ninja.

During the 1660s, Shaolin-style martial arts were introduced by the Chinese military attache, Kong Shang-Kung (or Kushanku as he was known to the Okinawans). Later, Chinese military attaches added to the knowledge of unarmed combat already gained by the Okinawans. When the Shogun placed a ban on the use of all weapons by the locals—only the famed Japanese samurai were allowed to bear arms—the practice of unarmed martial arts increased in popularity.

The already ancient Okinawan tradition of *te*, the martial art of the hand, had by this time reached a high peak of excellence, and the masters of the art were able to simulate, with their bare hands, all the effects of known conventional weapons. They were, indeed, convinced that the decision to ban the carrying of all weapons was, in effect, an act of great wisdom and not at all restrictive. During the latter part of the nineteenth century, the Japanese finally instituted full and effective control over Okinawa and were cruelly harsh on anyone who disputed their authority. This rigid attitude contributed indirectly toward the secret development of the martial arts by the native Okinawans. Karate, as it is known today, probably the most widespread and popular of all martial arts forms that have found their way to the West, represents a synthesis of the original Okinawan te fighting art (or *to-de* as it later became known) and the Chinese Shaolin tradition.

The word karate can be interpreted in two different ways: The most popular usage today is "empty hand;" the original meaning was "China hand" (the Japanese character *kara* can mean either "China" or "empty"). Empty hand is perhaps most contemporarily descriptive, in that it conveys the fact that karate, as it was initially conceived, was basically a weaponless martial art. The essence of success in karate involves agility, endurance, and co-ordination of all the faculties—physical, mental, intuitive/reflexive, and spiritual. It is also a superb system for achievement of physical fitness and, in particular, for mastery over body and mind.

Some claim that karate is the ultimate art of violence. By its nature it is a method of attack that relies primarily on the employment of striking blows, using fists, feet, knees, elbows, head, any part of the body available.

Ritualistic patterns

All three of the original Okinawan schools followed their own strict ritualistic patterns, in preparation and in training, and to this day the philosophical influence of Zen Buddhism is ever-present within the walls of any karate dojo. The dojo, or training hall, is considered sacred ground and has become almost a place of worship. A special feature is the shrine, usually displaying a picture of Bodhidharma, the canny Indian monk who founded Shaolin k'ung fu (he is known as Dharuma in Japan). Training sessions generally begin with the karate-kas, or students, sitting in rows and bowing before the shrine and to the dojo master. The etiquette of karate is treated with as much importance as the actual practice of the katas, or forms.

Outside the dojo, it is not unusual to see a set of carved Okinawan lions, a reminder of the fighting form's origins, one with snarling, open mouth and exhaling, the other with closed mouth, inhaling.

8 ☯ The ultimate martial art?

My head is hard as my pillo
But when my head feels the pillo of my love
I lose my head completely

Kuroda Yoshitaka

In ancient days, the wives of Japanese bushi warriors—
who preceded the samurai as Japan's warrior class—
learned to defend themselves with a weapon known as
the *naginata*. This consisted of a pole of about four feet in
length, with an ultra-sharp, three-feet long curved blade
at one end. The naginata was used as a battlefield
weapon for over a thousand years. It could out-reach a
normal sword, and was quite devastating when employed in a swift, sweeping motion. Training in the handling of the naginata was considered an essential part of
any young woman's upbringing.

So, too, was proficiency in the wielding of another,
far more gentle weapon, namely the bedroom pillow.

The Japanese word *shindai* means both "bed" and
"pillow-fighting." The ancient "marital art" of shindai
takes place only in the bedroom and is revered in Japan as
the ultimate solver of domestic disputes—which certainly
elevates it into something of a magickal martial art.

Fighting code

In the traditional scenario, shindai is only to be practiced between accredited love partners. The only weapons to be used are a pillow apiece, the battle arena is the bed—the bigger the better—and bearing in mind that the Japanese sleep on a futon on the floor, not on beds raised a foot or more above the floor. Also, in Japan, most walls through which a partner may be driven during a shindai bout are made of non-lethal rice paper. Through controlled pillow-fighting (shindai has its own very strict set of rules), couples are able to let off excess steam, and settle their domestic differences—before partaking in the ultimate "magickal ritual."

The shindai fighting code is very clearly defined, and despite the "soft" character of the "weapons," it can develop into quite a rough-and-tumble business. Even the size and shape of the regulation shindai pillow is constant, now based on the rules laid down by a Lady Hundra in 1908. Lady Hundra's shindai "code of conduct" contains such injunctions as: "No one may strike a second blow until the first blow has been returned"; "A tally shall be kept in the bedding cupboard showing the date and winner of each fight"; "No loss of face shall accompany the loser, nor shall the winner or the loser ever be proclaimed outside the household"; and "Every blow shall be accompanied by an expression of apology" (standard apologies include: "Shitsurei!"—literally "Sorry!"—and "Arigato!"—"Thank you (for trying to knock my block off)."

There are dozens of combat rules and pillow techniques. The end purpose of any shindai bout is to reach a so-called "point of reconciliation," and this final act of getting together is also performed according to a strict set of rules once the original dispute between partners that started the whole thing going has long since been forgotten.

Some rules of the shindai combat

For the use of any reader who may desire to try the delights of Japanese bed-fighting, perhaps as a prelude to tantric-type activity, we list some of the more important, stylized blows (the rest can be left to the imagination). The Japanese, it must be noted, have, down the years, been rather secretive about their "ultimate martial art," and there is a minimum of literature extant on the subject, even in the Japanese language. The only English book we have found on the subject is the excellent *Shindai: The Art of Japanese Bed Fighting* by Ellen Schumaker and the late Tomi Nobunuga.* The last named is described as "one of the great Shindai Mistresses of Japan," and the book is apparently the first attempt to ever record many of the secrets of the art, in either Japanese or English.

In Japan, it is apparently possible to purchase special "male" and "female" pillows marked with separate symbols denoting the sex of the potential combatant. These must be feather-filled and a small criss-cross gash is made in the pillow prior to use—traditionally this is done using an eider quill or wing feather. After the fight, and its potentially enjoyable postscript, comes the job of gathering up the loose feathers.

---

* London: Wolfe Publishing Limited (1965).

The main rule is to use the pillow only to strike an opponent, and not to use any part of the body. Music can be played in the background, if desired. It is also essential to choose a subject for discussion during the pillow fight that is totally unrelated to whatever subject is the current bone of contention leading up to the need for the shindai bout. There are a set of shindai "cries" to remember for use during the bout. The main ones are:

"Shitsurei!" ("Sorry!"),
   for use when striking a blow.
"Arigato!" ("Thank you!"),
   by the recipient of the blow.
"Maitta!" ("You've got me!"),
   when being smothered by an opponent's pillow.

These "cries" should be made loudly, with their source the lower abdomen (seat of the hara).

The pillow should be held on the sides, a couple of inches from the top seam, and not at the top. The aim is to try and strike your opponent with the "cutting edge" of the pillow, and to aim each blow at a particular spot on the body. It is never recommended to raise the pillow above the head, thus leaving the body open to attack. Most blows are made by swinging the pillow from either the right or left side. Before starting the bed fight, the two protaganists must first bow to each other while standing, and say words something like: "May the feathers decide which one of us is in the right, and may the other accept the choice." The pillows are then placed side by side on the floor and the opponents kneel behind them, still facing each other, and bow low until their heads touch the pillows in front of them, with arms stretched upward and backward. They then rise to face each other, about "twenty-six thumbs" apart. The fight starts with the male participant exclaiming "Hajimari-mas!" ("Let it begin!").

Shindai: the art of bed fighting.

According to Madame Nobunuga, the major selected target areas are: ear-hole, nostrils, mouth, armpit, fingers, shinbone, back of knee-joint, ankle, and elbow-joint ("funny bone"). The objective is also to try and knock an opponent off-balance. In fact, all the normal precepts of regular martial arts combat apply; such as balance, economy of movement, going with the flow, and using the opponent's own strength and momentum as a weapon.

Leaps upward and backward jumps to avoid being hit are recommended, as is a rotating motion of the body in preparation for making a blow. An opponent's pillow may be caught in the mouth (and ripped open to release the feathers). If one of the combatants loses their pillow, the contest is generally considered won. However, the choice can be made to continue fighting by holding a single feather in each hand—which must be dislodged for a win to be recorded. Other ways of deciding the outcome include: the total exhaustion of one of the combatants; when all the feathers are knocked out of one pillow (leaving a "useless" weapon); if both partners are prostrated by spontaneous sneezing; or if one partner (who becomes the loser) is "knocked through the dividing wall of the room."

Finally, the loser must prostrate him/herself before the winner in total humility, and beg forgiveness. The routines of the proceeding final act of reconciliation are not recorded by Madame Nobunuga.

If shindai does not quite represent the ultimate in martial arts activity, it certainly is one of the most pleasurable of the arts, and also carries with it enough magick of a rather special and enjoyable kind, especially in its concluding ritual, to warrant mention in this book. There

could, indeed, be certain suggestions here of a close connection with mystical sex magick practices that form part
of the Shinto and other ancient religious and philosophical
systems, a prime example being tantra yoga.

Tantric overtones

The yoga discipline falling loosely under the heading
"tantra" originated in India thousands of years ago, and
then spread to Tibet, China (where it was brought into
Taoistic magickal systems), and other places. Briefly put,
its ultimate aim is to arouse *shakti* or the feminine aspect
of universal energy, sometimes through ritual forms of
intercourse that embrace meditation and the withholding
of orgasm, especially by the male partner. In Taoistic
alchemical practice, it is thought desirable to create a so-
called "diamond body" to take over from the physical
body as a vehicle of the spirit. This is said to be achievable
through controlled mingling of male and female sexual
ch'i energies. Tantric concepts have been maintained
within the Japanese martial arts context by their link with
the practice of Shingon Mikkyo Buddhism, in which sexual and other desires are considered a vital source of energy. The Western Magickal Tradition has also been
profoundly influenced by tantric practices, as a form of
sex magick aimed at raising of the divine female Kundalini power through the chakras. This female energy is
thought to be the productive or inventive force of the
Divine creative power.

The exact origins of tantra are lost in the mists of
time, but are probably connected with early fertility practices, and the discovery of the potency of male/female

energies when brought together into mystical alignment. Most of Indian culture, especially art and architecture, have been influenced by the tantric tradition. Sensual sculptures depicting this essentially erotic but highly disciplined system for attaining higher consciousness can be seen adorning countless buildings around the Indian subcontinent, and in other Asian countries. In these representations of the sexual act, such coupling between male and female is considered as tantamount to union with the Divine, the ecstatic bliss of orgasm being viewed as a means of releasing the soul in the godhead. Some tantric sex rituals involve the reaching of nirvanic bliss through redirection of the sexual fluids back into the sadhaka (male) and sakti (female) participants.

Tantric ceremony and sexual practices vary from one school to another. Various versions have reached the West and are easily available in the form of literature and structured courses. What is continually stressed in tantric texts is the need for sincerity, dedication, and self-control, so that the practice of tantra yoga does not degenerate into mere gratification of sexual desires in the guise of spiritual practice.

In any event, tantra yoga or Taostic sexual practices cannot be considered to be solely linked with sexual energy manipulation, but also include the controlled use of all types of universal (or ch'i) energy. As one example from the martial arts, in ninjutsu occult lore there are considered to be five basic forms of energy within tantra, roughly categorized under the headings: intelligence, awareness, passion, action, and creation. The ultimate object in any tantric exercise is to attain a point of samadhi or enlightenment, a state of not just *knowing* Divine wisdom, but of *being* Divine wisdom. This aim of allowing the spirit (some may prefer to use the term mind) to motivate the physical is, of course, very similar to that of the traditional Oriental martial artist, being very much influenced by the early Chinese Taoistic philosophical and magickal systems. These systems, in turn, have a considerable portion of their foundations firmly set in the Indian/Tibetan tantric traditions, even if, strictly speaking, there may be today no direct link between the marital martial art of shindai and tantric practices.

9 ☯ Moving with the wind

A selection of martial arts exercises

Technical knowledge is not enough. One must
transcend techniques so that the art becomes
an artless art, growing out of the unconscious.

Daisetsu Suzuki

The stiff and unbending is the disciple of death.
The gentle and yielding is the disciple of life.
Thus an army without flexibility never wins a battle.
A tree that is unbending is easily broken . . .

Lao-tzu
Tao te-Ching

One of the earliest philosophical influences over the martial arts came from the sixth century B.C.E. teachings of Lao-tzu, the founder of Taoism and author of the celebrated *Tao-te Ching*. Lao-tzu quoted the example of the tree which bends with the wind in a storm, and thus can survive nature's fiercest onslaughts. He proposed that those who rely on the strength of their own force alone do not ultimately conquer. With a few exceptions, to this very day, the main emphasis in many of the practical martial arts is placed on flowing with the force of one's attacker, and using his/her own strength to overcome him/her.

This emphasis on "movement" is, perhaps, one of the most fundamentally important aspects of martial arts practice. It is also another possible future linking factor between Eastern and Western spiritual systems.

Movement, in effect, creates the essential connection with the spirit, with some exceptions, as in certain exercises involving gathering together of ch'i energy.

In the Eastern practice of yoga and related external/internal systems of consciousness development, a connection is usually made with energies more subtle than the physical, when in the sitting position, such as when meditating or conducting a specified mantra ritual while in the well-known "lotus" or similar postures. In contrast, in the Western religious and magickal traditions, such a connection (both real and symbolic) is normally achieved while in a standing position. The ultimate source of the energies contacted remains, however, the same for both.

Yoga and other practitioners gain the ability to make the higher-level connection by becoming physically and psychically sensitive, by dint of specialized exercise techniques. In the West, the general practice has become to use archetypal and other symbols in the form of ritual as a "switch," to turn contacts on and off, and without necessarily having to go through the whole process of personal body attuning. Moreover, Eastern techniques usually relate to a "raising of the power," as in the so-called kundalini experience, while in most Western magickal practice, the originally Middle Eastern Hebrew tradition of "calling the power down" is followed. (We have previously dealt with this subject in our book *Words of Power: Sacred Sounds of East and West*. St Paul: Llewellyn, 1991.)

What many of the Western spiritual practitioners have not borrowed from their Middle East sources is a proclivity for dance and movement; demonstrated, for example, in the mystical rituals of the Jewish Hassidim—which involve swaying and bowing, and also dance, as important methods of attaining *kavannah,* or complete mental and spiritual immersion in the divine—and the Muslim/Sufi whirling dervishes, whose movements range from the slow and almost hypnotic, to the superbly controlled frenzied. One must also not overlook the unique dancing forms that are an essential part of the sacred practices of the aboriginal peoples of the planet, such as, for example, the many African tribes, native Australians, and native North Americans. In Asian countries, in particular, the art of ritual dancing has been developed into a very high form of communication with subtle energies.

Yehuda Tagar, Israeli-born originator of the system of body/soul harmony known as Philophonetics, describes the body as ". . . an instrument of meaning, forming inner life in outer space." (For the record, Philophonetics combines movement and sound in a subtle experiential and therapeutic combination, and is now taught as part of several tertiary and other educational courses in Australia.) Tagar has based most of his teaching theories on the work of the noted mystic Rudolf Steiner, and Steiner's own references to "movements arising out of the being of man" and "the outpouring of the soul

---

* *Eurythmy as Visible Speech* (London: Rudolf Steiner Press, 1931), pp. 157 and 188.

into form and movement"* may be quite suitably applied to the martial arts. Thus, the intuitively mobile martial arts routines, based as they are on esoteric as well as functional foundations, may offer the West an important way of initiating or enhancing mystical experience through movement, so as to create a connection with this "inner life." This could occur both as a complement to more stationary ritual activities, and in addition to merely providing a method of improved vitality and health on all levels, through martial arts-type activity.

Anyone who has trained for any particular sport will agree that the ultimate aim of dedicated practice is to attain such "form" as to be able to move at ease in any given sporting situation, without consciously thinking about what move to make. Of what benefit might it not be if the same could be applied to our spiritual lives?

"Moving with the wind" is not merely an automatic response, it is a response of fulfillment.

The exercise routines offered below are based on regular martial arts routines taken from several different disciplines. They should be viewed as a first experience only, for use by any reader who wishes to sample for him/herself the physical, mental/psychical, and spiritual benefits to be obtained from "moving with the wind." Anyone who wishes to partake in the full richness of the many forms of movement available within any particular martial arts system is directed toward one of the accredited teachers of that system. Mastery of the martial arts requires much time, repeated doing, and an endless patience and dedication that must border on devotion. There is simply no easy road to success. It is essential to repeat that, without direct input by an accredited tutor of any chosen type of fighting art, there remains doubt that an individual would be able to fully absorb the many nuances that make up the magick of the martial arts.

As will no doubt be noted by anyone who tries them, the exercises presented here commence with several rather more stationary, preparatory-type routines, but flow progressively into a set of more active movements. All have been specially adapted for the beginner from routines used by martial artists of the East over the centuries, both for improvement of their general physical capability as related to combat skills, and, more importantly, to initiate essential contact with the inner self.

A critical element to hold in mind when performing any martial arts stance or movement is that all movement should be done from the hara, the energy collective point about two inches below the navel (see Exercise 1 below), with balance shifting from the hip and not from the shoulders. This is not always easy to do without direct instruction.

Exercise 1: Ch'i and the art of breathing

The concept of ch'i—the eternal, universal force—is not exclusively related to the martial arts. Yoga or Zen-type meditation and breathing techniques can be used to stimulate ch'i and encourage its flow through an individual's system, for a variety of uses and benefits, from healing through energy for action. Mental training, or the art of stilling the mind, is a foundation block of yoga, Zen, and martial arts practice, and an essential component in stimulating ch'i. The other essential element involved (apart from mental visualization) is proper breathing.

The process of breathing, in Eastern terms, includes not only the taking of adequate air to the lungs, but also the circulation of life-promoting oxygen throughout the body, through the agency of the blood. When breathing in deeply, it is most beneficial to take the inhalation, not only into the lungs, but as if carrying it deep into the abdomen. Ch'i, borne on the breath, is said to be collected at a point about two inches (three fingers) below the navel—known to the Chinese as *t'an tien* (or ch'ien) and the Japanese as *hara*. Once the hara is filled with the life-bearing force, from its point below the navel the ch'i can be "willed" to permeate throughout the body, simply by visualizing it circulating to the extremities of the limbs, like an early-morning fog creeping through city streets.

The following is a suggested starting ch'i energizing exercise based on several sources, and should ideally be done while standing erect, or sitting comfortably in a straight-backed chair, with legs apart at about shoulder width. Before starting, first memorize the exercise, it being essential not to disturb its flow by thinking too much about what comes next.

1. Still the mind: Begin breathing normally, in and out through the nostrils, and while doing so, listen intently to the sound of the breath, until all else is excluded from conscious thought, and the normally chattering mind is stilled.

2. Collecting ch'i: Change the breathing pattern, inhaling more deeply through the nostrils, causing the abdomen to expand, and then exhaling through the mouth, while drawing the abdomen back in.

The breath and ch'i.

This is all accomplished through the action of the diaphragm. All the time, keep the mind focused on the ch'i point two inches below the navel and feel the universal energy collecting there on each in-breath. Do this 20, 30, 50, 100 times—whatever is comfortable. (Special Note: As an alternative, when breathing in deeply, move the arms slowly upward and outward, like the wings of a bird, and then, during the out-breath, place one hand atop the other with palms down, meeting just in front of the forehead, and press downward to the full extent of the arms, while expelling the breath, and tensing the abdomen muscles. Then relax and repeat on the in-breath.)

3. Distributing ch'i: While continuing deep-breathing as in 2, when breathing out, feel the ch'i energy flowing through the body to the tips of the fingers and toes: to the top of the head; permeating every organ, every muscle and bone; and radiating out over the skin. The whole system becomes charged and revitalized.

4. Storing ch'i: Slowly revert back to a normal breathing pattern, and while doing so, visualize the ch'i energy flowing back toward its storehouse below the navel, to be kept for use whenever needed in daily life.

Exercise 2: Horse stance

In several k'ung fu schools, the so-called "horse stance," or *ma-pau*, with its many variations, is one of the central exercises, both for strengthening the legs and back, and for the development of controlled physical balance that can ultimately lead to controlled emotional, mental, and spiritual balance. (Horses have, incidentally, always been closely associated with magick, and are considered to enjoy special clairvoyant powers.)

Side benefits include general improved blood circulation and digestive capacity, and an end to any constipation problems. Also of great importance is the fact that it is virtually impossible in combat to shift anyone who has perfected the horse stance as a fighting stance.

Legend tells us that the old masters of k'ung fu would have their pupils practice the horse stance for up to three years before deciding if they would teach them further.

To perform this exercise, preferably wear flat-soled shoes and loose fitting garments.

1. Point of balance: Stand erect, and then begin shifting the feet sideways, to "open" the stance until a "perfect point of balance" is found—usually about two foot-lengths each side of a central line that extends downward from the crown of the head.

2. Sitting in the saddle: Clench the fists, and bending the elbows, bring the fists into line with the waist. Keeping legs apart, with toes pointing forward,

begin to bend the knees until a comfortable "sitting position" is found, without losing balance. Remember to keep the back straight, with the head erect, and the eyes looking straight ahead. The stomach should be flat, and, viewed from the side, the back of the head and the entire upper body will be in a straight line.

3. Holding the position: Breathing normally, hold this position as long as possible, listening to the sound of your breathing. A couple of minutes the first time around would be excellent. As the legs strengthen, it will become possible to hold the horse stance for a longer period, and as balance improves, the original position can be made lower.

Special note: As with the "ch'i exercise" above, the horse stance can be used to collect chi force into the lower abdomen.

Once the horse stance has been reasonably mastered, and becomes a comfortable and easy exercise, in balance—and in tune—with the theory that connection comes with movement, try changing position without disturbing the balance.

For instance, by straightening one knee while keeping the other bent, and alternating knees, a rhythmic sequence can be initiated. Also, by beginning with one foot placed ahead of the other on a horizontal line, a similar motion can be initiated. Again, after a while, alternate leg positions.

Additional variations might involve the shifting of weight from toe to heel, all the time remembering that the keeping of balance is of prime importance.

The horse stance.

Exercise 3: Fighting stance

A whole series of set standing stances make up the platforms from which a karate exponent can move into action. There are a wide number of stances, one for every possible eventuality—which means that, ideally, a karate-ka should never be caught off guard, or off balance. Stances are never rigidly held. Speed of change is always vital. Three elements are involved— length, width, and height of stance. A long stance provides stability moving forward or backward. A wide stance ensures balance. A low stance provides a lower center of gravity. A high stance can be used as a starting point for high-kicking and other moves that require speed and mobility.

In any karate dojo, the command "yoi" will be given for karate-ka to change from one stance to another. Other than their use as fighting platforms, karate stances are also designed for toning of muscle and strengthening of the entire bodily system—again as preparation for toning of the other faculties, including the intuitive. A few of these stances are noted below for those readers who would like to get the feel of karate's first principles.

A cautionary note is that no violent striking moves should ever be attempted without first warming up. Extra care should also be taken not to allow the elbow to lock at the end of any motion. If done improperly or too vigorously, there is danger of elbow tendon damage.

1. Musubi-dachi (the attention stance): Stand erect, back straight, and head held high. Keep the chin

The fighting stance.

down, but look straight ahead. Heels should be together. Hands are held loosely at the sides, palms lightly touching the thighs. Weight should be concentrated on the lower part of the body, with stomach muscles relaxed. Breathing should be normal.

2. Hachiji-dachi (the ready stance): (This stance is assumed from stance 1.) In a single movement, open up the feet to a comfortable width—with the outside of the feet about shoulder width, and toes turned slightly outward—and close the fists, straightening the arms, and holding them slightly away from the body. A simple movement of one foot leading the body can alter the position to meet that of any attacker, or aid in presenting a narrower target. Breathing should be measured, ready to call on the ki energy.

3. Kokatsu-dachi (the back stance): From stance 2, move the left foot forward a pace, toes pointing forward, but keeping the body's weight firmly on the back foot. Then immediately proceed to step 4.

4. Chudan-uchiuke (forearm block): With elbow bent, bring the left fist up (as if in an undercut punch— palm upward, but fist clenched) in a blocking movement. As part of the movement, expel breath sharply, using the "kiai" shout. Follow immediately with step 5.

5. Gyaku-zuki (reverse punch): Take a quick breath and, without changing the basic stance, execute a right reverse punch (fist clenched; palm down),

drawing the left arm back to original position, alongside body, and again expelling air using the "kiai" shout.

Exercise 4: Purifying ritual

Many tai ch'i, k'ung-fu, and other martial arts routines are based on the movements of one animal or another (see Chapter 4). This emphasis on the simulation of motions made by an animal suggests a totemistic link, and brings into the fighting disciplines a certain shamanistic flavor more in keeping with ritual and magick than with the art of combat. The following routine is based on a tai ch'i exercise known as "white crane cools its wings." It is a relaxing and purifying ritual that helps to revivify body, mind, and psychical aura, just as the crane will relax and cool its wings after a long flight. It should be done at slow speed, with the body relaxed, but still alert, as would be that of a bird which senses no immediate danger and is happily preening itself, but ready for swift flight or action should the need arise.

1. Facing north, stand loosely erect, relaxed, with arms at sides, feet about twelve inches apart. Now move into the routine, going from one position to the other slowly, but without stopping (it may be necessary to practice this exercise a few times to get into the flow of things).

2. Bow from the waist, at the same time raising the right hand, palm open and facing outward, level

with the chin, while dropping the left arm, with the left hand also open and level with the left knee, palm facing downward.

3. Keeping the hands in the same positions, swivel the body at the waist, moving to the left. Now raise the left hand to come into line with the right hand, about the width of the face apart, both palms still open, just above eye/nose level. (Keep your balance throughout. If at any time you lose your balance, start over, and keep trying.)

4. Keeping the hands in front, in line with the head, palms out, raise the body, straightening until erect.

5. Still holding the hands up and facing outward on either side of the head, turn the body back to face north again, as in the starting pose.

6. Drop the hands slightly, palms still facing outward, until the fingertips are level with the eyes.

7. Bend the knees slightly, while turning the still-open right hand inward and sideways, so that the palm is turned toward the face, and the thumb projects upward.

8. Lower the arms, and straighten up into the comfortable opening posture—and then start the exercise all over again (repeat 7 times).

Commencement of the purifying ritual stance.

The Kyudo archer

There is a saying in the traditional *Manual of Zen Buddhism* which states: "Even when greeted with swords and spears it (Zen) never loses its quiet way." Of all the martial arts that display a distinctive esoteric nature, *kyudo*, "the way of the bow," is at once one of the most magickal, and a typical example of Zen in action. In the traditional Ogasawara school manner, when the *kyudoka* (one who practices kyudo) draws his/her bow, or *yumi*, there is no opponent to face; only the kyudoka's own self needs to be conquered. As a form of archery vastly different in its aims from anything known in the West, genuine kyudo has little to do with hitting a bull's-eye, or even the target. It is, in its deepest sense, a masterly form of meditation. The string is only loosed once the mind has entered those regions of meditation that form part of the unteachable Zen doctrine (or non-doctrine). The only vital part in the act of letting the string go is the action itself. The fact that the arrow might actually hit the target is of secondary consequence. Style and method are more significant to the archer than a mere target. The state of mind at the moment the arrow is released remains most important of all.

The kyudo bow, the yumi, is an enormous affair, some six-feet long and made from strips of laminated wood—much longer even than the famous English longbow of the Middle Ages. The kyudo archer grips his yumi about one-third of the way from the bottom and goes through eight distinctive movements, known as *hassetsu*, before the shot is completed. Each of the initial steps, from the first, the *ashibumi* or "stepping into stance," to the sixth, the kiai, "the meeting between bowman and bow," prepares the kyudoka for that important moment when the arrow shoots itself—the "moment of release," the seventh movement, called the *hanare*.

The eighth stage, known as the *zanshin*—"the moment of knowledge"—sees the archer standing motionless as he/she watches the arrow winging its way into the distance. The performance is completed. Whether or not the arrow reaches the target is of no importance.

In full, the eight kyudo positions are:

1. Ashibumi—stepping into stance and positioning of the feet.

2. Dozukiri—steadying the body (this includes relaxed breath control).

3. Yugamae—setting the bow in place (the bow and arrow are still held down at the side).

4. Uchiokoshi—lifting and looking (simultaneously the bow is lifted and the target sighted).

5. Hikiwake—the draw.

6. Kiai—the meeting or union.

7. Hanare—moment of release.

8. Zanshin—moment of knowledge.

An exercise for anyone to perform based on the eight-fold kyudo routine is given below. All eight stages must be approached with absolute precision, in a totally relaxed state, and with personal enlightenment as the ultimate result kept firmly in mind.

It is interesting to note the name of the sixth position, "the meeting between bowman and bow," is "kiai," which is the same as given to the famous karate kiai "shout of power."

Meditative and magickal-type ritual not only surrounds the actual shooting of the arrow, but is also observed in the manufacture of the bow and its accompanying missiles. Cut only around the time of the winter solstice, the arrows are left to dry for three months. Only the very straightest bamboo cane is selected, and of a type that will emit the correct sounds for chasing away evil spirits. The size of the arrow is very important and will generally embody some element of the number eight. In Japanese Shinto tradition, the figure 8 signifies the complete circle of infinity. White eagle or falcon feathers are attached to the first arrow to be released, to immediately ward off evil spirits, who, being of a dark nature, are frightened by the color white.

A spectacular variation of the art of kyudo is performed from horseback and is known as *yabusame*. Annual yabusame contests are held at Shinto shrines all around Japan. The archers gallop along a 280-yard course, controlling their mounts with their knees, and shoot at evenly-spaced targets set up on poles. Contestants dress up in colorful, ancient samurai costumes to commemorate the antiquity of their art and observe strict ceremonial rites designed to create a bonding between human and cosmic forces.

Central to the meditative practice of Japanese kyudo archery is the concept of ki (ch'i)—the fundamental energy of the universe—as the principle factor to be used for unification of body and mind in a single process. Body and mind are two separate entities, but the mind controls the body, directing ki (which obeys the mind) to motivate the body, as required, and at any given time. As we have already noted, the vital point on the body that acts as a motivation point for ki, and a kind of essential energy reservoir, is located just below the navel, and is known in Japanese as the hara. The center of the hara is known as *seika-no-itten,* the "vital point." It is the spot where, in a psychical or spiritual sense, the combined energy essence of body and mind converge. It is the activation of this true "center of equilibrium" that determines true mental and physical coordination.

Exercise 5: Zen in action—the kyudo archer

The eight staged movements made by a kyudo archer may be used to simulate the act of shooting a bow without actually using any bow and arrow at all. More important than having an actual weapon in hand is the mental attitude of the bowperson. In the end result, there is no need for a target.

In order to do this exercise it will be necessary to first study carefully the "horse stance" exercise given earlier, as elements of this form the basis of the kyudo archer routine.

Before starting the exercise, read and absorb all of the instructions given below, so that there will be no need to think too hard about them after a few tries. The object is to eventually perform the exercise as a moving meditation, without the conscious mind intruding. Then follow this routine:

1. Stepping into stance: Take up a "half-horse" position similar to (but not as deep as) that described in the "horse stance" exercise. Avoid a posture that causes any strain, as it will have to be kept for the duration. If the horse stance is found to be too difficult to hold while simulating the kyudo movements, do the exercise standing up straight, but with knees slightly bent and legs apart.

2. Positioning the body: Place the hands on upper thighs, palms down, and begin to breathe, slowly, rhythmically.

3. Setting the bow in place: While breathing in, raise the right arm sideways to shoulder height and then, with eyes following the line of flight, focusing on the nail of the middle finger, and while breathing out, swing the right arm slowly in a circle, across and in front of the body at eye level, until the right hand is pointing along a line almost level with the left shoulder.

4. Lifting and looking: Holding the breath awhile, raise the left arm until the left hand meets the right hand. Now sight the imaginary target. Breath out and . . .

5. The draw: Breathing in again, and without losing sight of the imaginary target, draw the right hand back, as if priming the string of a bow, with the left hand remaining in the position it would be to normally hold a bow.

The Kyudo archer stance.

6. The meeting: Holding the breath awhile, stay in this archer's pose, sighting the target. Then begin breathing softly again, but hold the pose, as if in meditation.

7. Moment of release: The arrow shoots itself as the right hand opens on an out breath.

8. Moment of knowledge: Breathing normally, drop both hands back to your thighs as you turn your head to look straight ahead, without even wondering as to whether your arrow has reached its target or not.

Rest for a moment in this pose, and then repeat the exercise, this time starting with the left hand.

Holistic response

For anyone who cares to do so, and in tune with the overtones of universal validity, the eightfold way of kyudo may easily be applied as eight basic steps for a holistic response on the esoteric or mind level, not only in the martial arts context, but in meeting any situation in life. Suggested stages are:

1. By "stepping into stance" a person moves into the best possible position to face whatever has to be faced (be it on the physical, mental, or paraphysical planes).

Then follows:

2. A relaxed appraisal of the situation ("steadying the body").

3. A gathering of forces ("setting the bow in place").

4. A sighting of the objective ("lifting and looking").

5. Preparation for action ("the draw").

6. Waiting for the appropriate moment or timing ("the meeting or union").

7. Direct action on whatever appropriate level ("moment of release").

8. Finally, success or illumination ("moment of knowledge").

Exercise 6: Centering the ki

The practice of the martial arts form known as aikido (see Chapter 5) is based on the use of fluid circular movements from a constant central point, which is controlled by the ki force. Just as the name aikido means "in harmony with the universe," so too do the movements inherent in most of its forms reflect the essential oneness of all matter, all experience. Aikidoists glide smoothly around the floor in almost choreographed style, much like expert dancers. The movement of the body simulates the movement of the center. It is believed that if the philosophy behind aikido were to be applied in all areas of human activity, there would result a smoothly operating society, with a firm, but fluid and flexible, central control based on full compatibility with cosmic law.

Of all the martial arts forms, aikido, in its purest variety, is acknowledged as possibly the most mystical (although the lesser known shorinji kempo may be considered to be on a par), and probably the most suited to those people seeking a spiritual path ahead of a mere combat form. The exercise which follows is known as *funakogi* boat-rowing.

1. Stand relaxed but alert, facing north, with arms hanging at sides, feet comfortably together.

2. Move the right foot forward, at the same time clenching the fists as if they were holding oars.

3. Now exchange feet—left forward, right back—while bringing the arms up, fists level with the top of the head, as if raising the oars.

4. Exchange feet again, right forward, left back, simultaneously bringing the arms down again to their starting position—lowering the oars.

5. Keep repeating, as smoothly as possible, twenty times or more if desired. The center point is the hips area. The rhythmic back-and-forth (feet), up-and-down (arms) movement (*furitama*—"ki settling") helps focus the ki/ch'i into this centrum.

10 ☯ Meditation and the martial arts

The one moon reflects itself
wherever there is a sheet of water

Manual of Zen Buddhism

In Western martial arts circles, attitudes toward meditation vary from acceptance of its necessity, to payment of
lip service to its practice—sometimes by way of patently
meaningless rituals before and/or after training—and
even downright rejection. According to one notable
source, in the practice of the near-mystical aikido some
primarily Western students "manage to progress without
involving themselves in the mental/spiritual side of the
subject."* We have also read several articles in martial
arts magazines in which the viewpoint is expressed that
the martial arts are essentially fighting systems, and that
their mystical side is virtually superfluous. However, if
one is to take any cognizance of the words of Morihei
Ueshiba, founder of aikido (namely)—"Through the subtle working of ki, mind and body are harmonized and the

---

* *Martial Arts of the Orient,* ed. Bryn Williams (London: Hamlyn, 1985), p. 124.

relationship between the individual and the universe is harmonized"*—it becomes evident that any truly serious practice of aikido must, by necessity, involve training of both the body and the mind—with the concept of ki thrown in as an inescapable spiritual additive.

And if what we, ourselves, have been told by several accredited Eastern masters of the arts has any bearing, the same applies for most, and probably all, of the other Oriental martial arts disciplines.

Meditation and purification

The one common factor in all of the martial arts of the East remains the use of meditation in training. Many masters of the arts have been known to spend months, and even years, in solitary mountain or forest retreats, alone in meditation all day, receiving inspiration to be put into practice at a later stage. In the Japanese Shinto tradition, which influences so many of the martial arts systems of Japan and elsewhere, there is even a universal, yearly purification ritual, known as *misogi harai,* which consists of a holistic process ranging from clearing the body of toxins to clearing the mind and spirit through meditation.

There is really no great secret attached to the practice of meditation. It can be done anywhere at any time. Real adepts of the art are able to meditate on a moving bus or train, in a city apartment with street noises intruding from outside, or even in the midst of a noisy crowd at a football match. But, ideally, and for the beginner in any event,

---

* *The Spirit of Aikido,* p. 74.

meditation should be done in a quiet place. Martial artists have generally found it beneficial to meditate out-of-doors, particularly on a mountaintop or hilltop, in a forest, or overlooking a lake or the sea. Meditation is a marvelous tool to be used to focus and magnify ch'i energy, and also, usually at a later stage, as a prelude to communication with rarer realms of existence.

There are also no rigid guidelines relating to times for meditation, although early morning and just before retiring at night are suggested as appropriate times, for obvious reasons: morning meditation prepares a person for the day ahead; evening meditation ensures sound, restful, and health-enhancing sleep.

Specified breathing techniques of the yoga variety are also favored in martial arts training meditation, such as: alternate nostril breathing (using thumb and forefinger to open and close the nostrils alternately), used for balancing the body/mind energies; "observed" natural breathing (allowing the lungs to breathe with their own rhythm); and "ignored" breathing (a technique in which the autonomic nervous system is allowed to take over, after having breathed out and then purposefully not taken a conscious in-breath).

There are probably as many meditation techniques as there are martial arts masters (and pupils), and the following selection is offered for suggested use only.

Meditation 1: Vitalizing the body

Sit in a straight-backed chair, or cross-legged on a mat or carpet on the floor (in the lotus or half-lotus position, if able). If there is any difficulty in keeping the back straight while sitting crosslegged on the floor, sit adjacent a wall. Keep the feet flat on the floor, and the open hands cupped just below the navel. This hand position will immediately help to instill a feeling of relaxation. (Anyone who is in a particularly stressed state might like to first try the hand therapy exercise given in the shiatsu section under the heading "Calming the nerves" (see Chapter 11).

Breathing normally, take the mind's attention to the tan t'ien or hara ch'i/ki energy point three fingers below the navel, and hold concentration at that point for a few moments. Now move the attention to the kidney area, and again hold for a while. Next, move attention to the area between the base of the spine and the genitals, and again, hold for a few moments. Finally, take the mind right down to the soles of the feet, and remain thus in meditation for 10 to 15 minutes, or longer of desired.

At the end of the meditation (regular meditators find that the meditation has an uncanny knack of "timing itself"), bring the attention up again via the same route used at the start—and then back into the mind itself. Throughout the meditation, breathing should be slow but regular.

This meditation serves to energize the vital lower physical organs with ch'i energy.

Meditation 2: The seiza position

If able to, assume the traditional Japanese *seiza* (formal style of sitting) position—with hands placed flat on bended knees, and with back upright. This is the natural sitting posture used in most dojos (martial arts training halls) before and after a bout or set of exercise katas. From ancient times, practice of the martial arts has always begun and ended with this essential form of etiquette, with opponents facing each other on their knees, and bowing to each other as a sign of mutual respect. Their straightened backs symbolize their true intent of attaining spiritual enlightenment as an end result of their physical activity.

To get into the seiza position correctly, first take the left foot back half a step, and place the left knee on the floor. Then take the right foot back half a step and place the right knee on the floor, with the big toes touching each other and tops of feet flat on floor. Then lower the hips until the buttocks rest on the heels. Men must hold their knees two clenched fists apart, and women, one fist. The hands should rest lightly on the knees. Shoulders should be relaxed and down, with back straight, head erect (as if there were a plumb line entering at the crown), and eyes looking straight ahead, in order to close the body's energy circuit.

As this position is uncommon to westerners, it may take some while getting used to. Do not, under any circumstances, strain yourself doing it. If you feel your legs going numb, stop immediately, relax, and allow the bloodflow to return before rising. Try the position for limited periods of time at first, increasing as you go along. If you find the seiza position just too uncomfortable to bear, do the meditation sitting erect in a straight-backed chair.

Meditation: Breathing normally, close the eyes and take the attention to the hara point, three fingers below the navel. By an effort of will, raise the ch'i energy, seeing it as a bright white light, from the hara to the solar plexus area. Here it transforms into a bright yellow, healing light. Feel this light stilling the emotions that emanate from the solar plexus "chakra," one of the seven major bodily entry points for energy.

Now raise the ch'i energy to a central point in line with the heart. Here its color changes from yellow to emerald green. Hold for a moment, while bringing the beat of the human heart into alignment with the heartbeat of the cosmos. Next, raise the mental focus to the throat area, visualize it vibrating to the color turquoise. Hold again, while listening intently to the "sound of silence." Now take the attention to the center of the forehead, the seat of the so-called "third eye," the organ of clairvoyance (or "clear seeing on all levels"), as the ch'i energy transforms into the color royal blue. Hold for a while, using the royal blue light to clear the mind of all extraneous thoughts. Finally, raise the ch'i energy to the crown of the head, where it becomes purple in color. This is the entry point to subtler dimensions. Go into meditation for 5–10 minutes, while seeing the entire body become bathed in soft purple light.

The body's own time clock will normally indicate when it is time to come out of meditation. When this occurs, draw the purple-colored ch'i energy into the crown chakra, and then down again to the third eye position, where it is transformed into royal blue. Likewise, moving down through the other "chakra" positions, visualize a continuing change of color, as the ch'i descends back to the hara point: turquoise at the throat; emerald green at the heart; yellow at the solar plexus; and then white again at the hara.

As a closing protection, mentally project a stream of light—like a sword or needle—shooting out from the hara to a point about a foot in front of it. Use this point of light to mentally draw a circle of white light protection around the body, before withdrawing the needle of hara light. This special protection of the aura will remain until the next meditation session.

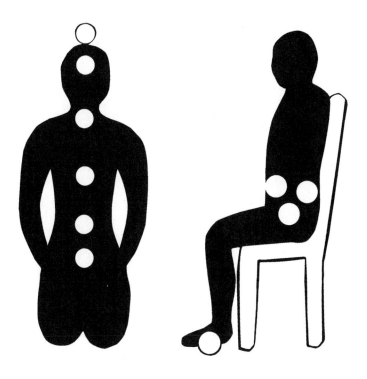

Vitalizing the body—Seiza positions used in meditations.

Mantras and mudras

A form of esoteric Buddhism brought to Japan from China by the priest Kukai (known in Japan as Kobo Daishi) at the beginning of the ninth century is known in Japanese as *Mikkyo*—meaning "secret teaching." Mikkyo, a division of Shingon Buddhism ("School of the True Word"), originated in India and is a synthesis of a variety of doctrines, philosophies, rituals, and meditation techniques. Kobo Daishi believed that every religion signified one of ten stages in humankind's progress to Buddhahood. An important aspect of Mikkyo practice is the use of mantra, or sacred sound, while placing the fingers of the two hands in certain pre-specified positions, known as mudras, in order to channel and direct essential energy.

The fingers of the right hand represent the inner manifestation, and those on the left hand the outer manifestation, of ch'i/ki energy. The left hand is regarded as yin (Japanese: *in*), representing passive absorption and truth; the right hand symbolizes yang (Japanese: *yo*), and signifies active visualization and wisdom. The five fingers of each hand are associated with the five elements: little finger = earth or ch'i; ring finger = water; middle finger = fire; index finger = air; thumb = space; the void. There are literally hundreds of mudra positions to be used for various reasons.

Certain of the mudras (*ketsu-in* in Japanese) and mantras (*jumon*) are known to have been used by the ninjas of old, and are, according to some reports, still used secretly today in modern ninja schools, and by some other martial artists. The sounds intoned while the hands are held in the nine mudra positions that make up the so-called *kuji no ho* ("nine syllable protection method"), may be termed an equivalent of the *bija* or seed sounds of mantra yoga tradition. The kuji no ho technique is used as part of a special meditation ritual, for protection and for energy revitalization on all levels. It is, however, virtually impossible to teach anyone via the written word how to attain these complicated hand positions while chanting the appropriate mantra. Moreover, ninja and other tradition affirms that the full secrets of correct mudra and mantra use can only be passed on directly from master to disciple. Thus, the meditation given below uses the nine mentioned sounds only. (Anyone who cares to try and attain the hand mudra positions as given in the accompanying illustrations may, however, want to try using the two techniques in unison.)

The sounds for, and names of, the nine hand positions, and their basic associations are:

1. Rin—strength.
2. Pyo—knowledge.
3. Toh—the universe.
4. Sho—the inner self.
5. Kai—awareness.
6. Jin—intuition.
7. Retsu—channelling (from a higher source).
8. Zai—attunement (with the ultimate).
9. Zen—the ultimate, clear state.

It would be a good idea to practice these sounds before attempting the simple meditation with sound given below, so as to be able to work easily with them without referring to the text.

Meditation 3: Meditation with sound

Sit in a quiet place, preferably on the floor, in a cross-legged lotus-type position, or in the martial arts way, hands flat on bended knees, with back straight, and head erect. Close the eyes.

Now chant:

RIN—and focus the attention on the ch'i energy point, about two inches below the navel. Feel the ch'i energy coursing through the body.

PYO—shift focus to the mind—the seat of knowledge—and feel the knowledge of the universe entering the consciousness.

TOH—extend attention out to the world—offering to share knowledge with all traveling companions on planet Earth, and on other planets in the universe.

SHO—move attention back to the inner self, at the heart center, and "listen" to the heartbeat synchronizing with the heartbeat of the universe.

KAI—focus on the ears, listening intently for the "voice of the silence" the voice of spiritual inspiration.

JIN—take the attention to the third eye region on the forehead—the seat of clairvoyant communication.

RETSU—move focus to the crown of the head—the entry point for communication from higher sources.

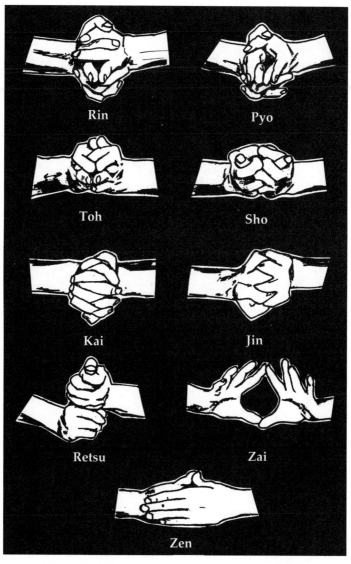

Meditation with sound: the nine kuji-no-in mudra positions.

ZAI—empty the mind, ready to receive.

ZEN—sit in the silence.

Hold the silence for as long as desired, and then move out of meditation by reversing the order of chanting, starting with ZEN and ending with RIN.

11 ☯ Healing arts

All things are backed by the Shade (yin)
and faced by the Light (Yang), and
harmonized by the immaterial Breath (ch'i).

Lao-tzu
Tao-te Ching

One nature, perfect and pervading,
circulates in all natures;

Manual of Zen Buddhism

One of the earliest of China's famous healers was the surgeon Hua T'o who lived in the second century, and who may even have preceded Bodhidharma as the founder of Chinese martial arts. According to legend, Hua T'o used his knowledge of medicine and the human body, plus observation of the movements of the deer, tiger, bear, monkey, and bird to create a system of health-giving exercises. The Chinese tradition of k'ung fu, in its "hard" and "soft" applications, is thus closely related to ancient methods of healing. This connection is also true of all of the other major martial arts forms, most of which incorporate at least some movements that are geared toward distributing ch'i energy to specified organs and areas of the body (particularly in the practice of ch'i-k'ung (see Chapter 2).

Healing and the martial arts

The fact that anyone involved in any of the fighting arts disciplines will, by necessity, be prone, from time to time, to accidental injury, has led to an intense interest in the healing arts among martial arts masters down the centuries. In the days before the appearance of doctor's surgeries and health clinics, the fighting academy or dojo master was expected to be able to handle the treatment of all forms of injuries, from simple strains, bruises, grazes, and cuts, to more complex muscle injuries and even dislocated or broken bones. A wide variety of methods and aids were used, including massage, chiropractic type manipulations, acupuncture, acupressure, plus hot baths, herbal remedies, and the like—in fact anything available from the traditional medicine chest of the country concerned. Thus, the knowledge gained in treating a large number of injuries and illnesses made the martial arts master the equal of any medical doctor of his time.

Western allopathic medicine views the body as having separate and distinct organ systems. In the East, a multiplicity of healing methods exist, mostly of a holistic nature, calling for a balancing of the energies of mind, body, and spirit, in order to attain good health. Feng shui practitioners of old would have added a fourth element: The disruption leading to any symptoms of disease might be any or all of physical, mental, psychical, *and* environmental.

Generally speaking, the accent in the Orient is as much on maintaining good health and achieving longevity as it is on the actual process of healing—with healing frequently only becoming necessary because a person has not chosen to observe basic health and fitness laws. The conviction is that correct physical, mental, and spiritual exercise will lead inexorably to near-perfect health, dispensing with the need for healers and physicians. This attitude may be termed particularly valid when associated with martial arts practice.

The paradox that sees the martial arts as both a method of self-defense and a form of spiritual development also applies in some areas of connected healing. For instance, the infamous dim muk "touch of death" or "vibrating palm" killer strikes used by masters of the iron palm technique (see Chapter 2) can also be utilized in a more positive fashion, to cure the sick and/or injured through application of ch'i by these highly specialized techniques of physical touch. (There may be some connection here between these techniques and the methods used by South American, Filipino, and other laying-on-of-hands healers around the world.)

As another example of a distinctive martial arts/ healing connection, the legend surrounding the fighting art of ju-jutsu concerns a famous Japanese physician, Akiyama. The wily Akiyama, it is told, transformed an ancient martial art form called *hakuda* into ju-jutsu after observing how an erect pine tree was destroyed during a violent snowstorm, while a willow tree survived because it yielded to the weight of the snow on its branches. A lesser-known, but very important, branch of ju-jutsu is called the art of *atemi*, teaching the application of pressure on certain vulnerable points on the body, by blow or kick, in order to immobilize or kill an opponent. However, as in the case of the vibrating palm technique in k'ung-fu, out of the deadly atemi there flows an ancient healing art. Known as *kuatsu*, this is a very effective method of resuscitation similar to shiatsu—the Japanese version of the Chinese acupressure system that uses various points on the body's so-called meridian system (see below), as for acupuncture—but using finger pressure instead of needles. Kuatsu-type techniques, it has been demonstrated, can be used to revive anyone incapacitated by suffocation, strangulation, or a severe blow.

The training of the dreaded ninja also did not overlook the value of such auxiliary skills as shiatsu and *junan-taiso*, the ninja's yoga-like, health-promoting, stretching and toning exercises. A form of self-healing was, indeed, an absolute necessity for any ninja, who would frequently operate many miles from a friendly base. Such healing generally involved some sort of shamanistic approach, combining "spiritual" healing—or channeling of ch'i/ki energy—plus expert knowledge of the use of selected healing plants, taken from whatever local environment the ninja happened to be in at the time. As a more deadly herbalistic sideline, in case of need, the ninja was also expected to become master of the art of concocting potions to poison another person or render him/her unconscious—and of corresponding antidotes.

The use of sound as a healing option (or even as a weapon) has already been touched on. It is of interest, however, to note here that, as part of the teachings they inherited from early Shingon Buddhists, ninjas were known to intone mantras (in Japanese: "jumon") for the channeling of subtle energies (see exercise below), and for various healing and revitalizing purposes.

(i) headache

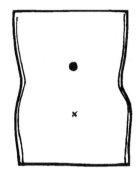

**(ii) indigestion and/or
stomach pain**

(iii) toothache

(iv) sore throat

Acupressure therapy points
(continued on next page)

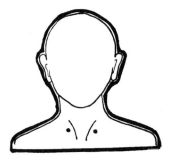

**(v) skin toning and
hormone stimulation**

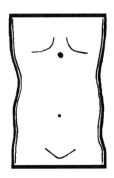

**(vi) improving sexual
performance**

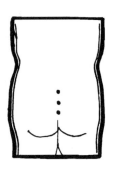

**(vii) improving sexual
performance**

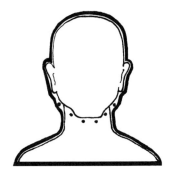

**(viii) improving sexual
performance**

Acupressure therapy points

Eight strands and twelve meridians

Traditional healing arts can be counted almost as old as humankind itself. One Chinese legend places the starting date of sophisticated healing techniques, such as acupuncture and herbal therapy, at around 10/12,000 years ago, when the so-called "Sons of Reflected Light" arrived in China. This was, according to the old tales, a race of people over seven feet tall, whose origin is unknown, but who handed on to the Chinese knowledge of many skills, before disappearing again a few centuries after their arrival, no one knows where. There have been claims that the classic Taoistic medical treatise known as (in its full title) *Huang Ti Nei Ching Su Wen* ("The Yellow Emperor's Classic of Internal Medicine") commonly called the *Nei Ching*—is based on techniques used by Emperor Hwang Ti around 3000 B.C.E., although its known written form appeared around 200-300 B.C.E. and appears to be a composite of the medical writings of numerous ancient physicians. (It is not to be confused with the equally extraordinary treatise known as the *Nei P'ing* written in 320 C.E. by the scholar Ko Hung, who broke the taboo against publishing Taoist oral traditions by compiling a fascinating mixture of secret alchemical magical, and psychophysical information, all bound with marvelous, erudite prose.)

Claims that Chinese medicine far outdates its Western counterpart in innovation and information are not based on hearsay. From many examples, as early as the third century C.E., Wang Shu-he wrote a treatise on pulse diagnosis, and in the sixteenth century Li Shi-jen catalogued more than 12,000 Chinese herbal medication recipes—activity that was far and away ahead of anything thus far produced in the West. As it stands, the over 2000-years-old *Nei Ching* supplies the basis of the eight major branches of the Chinese healing arts known as *pa chin hsien*, the "eight strands of the brocade." These are:

1. Natural dietary therapy (ch'ang ming)
2. Herbal therapy (ts'ao yao)
3. Heat treatment (wen chiech'u)
4. Massage (t'ui-na)
5. Acupuncture (hsia che'n pien)
6. Acupressure (tien che'n)
7. Physical exercise (t'i yu)
8. Ch'i control (ch'i-li nung)

Healing Exercise: Eight pieces of treasure

The Nei Ching suggests that certain bodily positions can have an effect on the internal organs. Interestingly, these exercises are known as the "Eight pieces of treasure," thus equating with the eight Japanese kyudo movements. Participation in these exercises also serves as a worthwhile introduction to the use of the ubiquitous ki or ch'i energy. Briefly put, the eight positions recommended in the *Nei Ching* and elsewhere for stimulation of the inner organs are:

1. "Two hands push up to the sky": Standing erect with feet apart and parallel to the shoulders, intertwine the fingers of the hands, with palms facing outward, and back of hands in line with the forehead. While inhaling deeply, push the hands and arms upward, simultaneously raising the heels to

stand on the toes, with arms ultimately at full stretch above the head (and with fingers remaining entwined). Hold a moment, then lower to first position while exhaling, bringing the heels back to the ground as in a single motion. (This exercise is said to stimulate the so-called "triple warmer" that controls body chemistry.)

2. "Drawing the bow": Starting with body erect and feet close together, take a wide step with the left foot until in a low position that simulates riding a horse. Raise the arms as if holding a bow in the right hand and an arrow in the left, and bring them to chest level in front of you, drawing the left arm back to prime the bow while inhaling. Exhale and come back to the starting erect position. Now repeat the exercise, reversing hand usage. (Enhances mental power, while also strengthening legs and arms).

3. "Alternate hand raising": Standing in a relaxed position with feet together, inhale while moving the left foot sideways to about shoulder width. Exhale. Inhaling again, raise the left arm to above the head, with open palm facing upward, while mentally directing the energy of the breath to the lower abdomen region. Exhale slowly while lowering the left hand and repeat using the right hand. (Vitalizes the spleen, stomach, and digestive system.)

4. "Looking backward": Stand erect with arms hanging loosely at sides, palms facing to the back, the feet about shoulder width apart, eyes forward, and

the tongue resting lightly on the palate. In a smooth single motion while breathing in, turn the head as far as possible to the left. Exhale while returning to the starting position, and then move the head to the right in similar fashion. (Stimulates the lungs and respiratory system.)

5. "Making fists": From the usual erect position, part the feet and lower the body as if sitting astride a horse. Inhaling, raise the arms to shoulder height in front of the body. Simultaneously, clench the fists and tighten the muscles of the anus, while mentally directing energy to a point just below the navel. All the time keep the eyes wide open and look straight ahead. Exhaling, return to starting position and repeat. (For the lower abdomen, sex organs, and to strengthen the eyes.)

6. "Rocking": Standing erect, feet slightly apart, shift the weight alternately to toes and then heels, in a rocking motion, while breathing normally. Keep the knees slightly bent. (Enhances blood flow and general vitality.)

7. "Rotating the head": Assume again the "horse-riding" position described above. Breathing normally, very carefully rotate the lower back and the head in a circle to the left. Repeat to the right. Try rotating the lower back in one direction and the head in the opposite direction. (Prevents heartburn and hiatal hernia, enhances digestion, and also strengthens the lower back and neck muscles.)

8. "Touching feet": Stand erect with feet a little less than shoulder width apart. Breathe in deeply to the abdomen, and while holding the breath, bend forward at the waist and try to touch the feet with outstretched finger tips. Return slowly to starting position and exhale slowly. (Warning: Not to be tried by persons with high blood pressure. Exercises the spinal column, and thus all of the connected internal organs.)

Special Note: it is recommended that each of the above exercise routines be performed eight times.

Healing magick at work

Traditional doctors also utilized the concepts of yin and yang and the five elements in their diagnoses, and usually opted for holistic cures that embraced any or all of the eight mentioned methods of healing. Central to all healing operations, and thought most important, was control of the ch'i energy, either through self-control exercises by the patient him/herself, or through the use of certain exterior stimuli, such as acupuncture needles or finger spot pressure.

According to the acupuncturist, it is an imbalance of the yin-yang ch'i forces distributed through so-called "twelve meridians" and "two vessels" in the body—the *ching-lo,* or energy paths—which brings on disease. In acupuncture, certain key points in these meridians are stimulated by the painless insertion of exceptionally thin, but very sharp needles, to a depth of about a tenth of an inch at various locations, each of which is directly connected with a limb and/or organ of the body via a meridian ch'i pathway. When an organ begins to malfunction because of inadequate flow of ch'i, the acupuncturist's needle placement will restimulate the flow of essential energy and thus rectify the problem. Acupuncture can also be used to relieve pain or to induce anaesthesia without drugs during an operation, or in the extracting of teeth. In ancient times, the acupuncturist's needles were made of flint, bone, or bamboo. Today, gold, silver, or stainless steel needles are used.

An impression of magic at work is created because the needles are usually inserted at points which have no apparent connection with the part of the body to be healed. There are over one thousand of these points for a practitioner of acupuncture to learn about. Each point bears its own name.

The *Nei Ching* teaches that correct flow of ch'i through the meridian paths is essential for the maintenance of harmonious body/mind/spirit balance. So, too, is the flow of blood (carrying nourishment via the veins and arteries), the continual natural moistening of tendons and bones, and the regulation of negative/positive yin/yang forces on all levels: physical, mental, and psychic. But all remain ultimately under the control of the ch'i. Six of the twelve basic acupuncture meridians are considered yang in nature—all placed on the outer side of the limbs; and six are yin in nature—all placed on the inner side of the limbs. Each meridian corresponds with some important, inner-organ function. The twelve, their positions and functions are:

yang meridians:
> arms—small intestine; "triple warmer"
> (controlling body chemistry); large intestine.
> legs—urinary system/bladder; gall bladder;
> stomach.

yin meridians:
> arms—lung; heart circulation (and sex);
> heart (organ).
> legs—liver; spleen/pancreas; kidney.

In addition to the twelve meridians, two "vessels" lie vertically midway between the two sides of the body, in front and back. These are: front—conception vessel; back—governing vessel.

Five elements and healing

The five elements also have specific associations connected with different types of healing. These can be calculated using certain astrological-type information taken from the patient's year, month, and day of birth. The element fire generally relates to a spiritual cure, wood to natural dietary therapy, earth to herbal therapy, metal to acupuncture, and water to heat therapy. The elements are also connected with the meridian organs, which have specified hours of peak activity. These connections are shown in the chart on the following page.

Elemental Healing Connections

Meridian	Element	Peak Hours
lung	metal	0300-0500
large intestine	metal	0500-0700
stomach	earth	0700-0900
spleen/pancreas	earth	0900-1100
heart	fire	1100-1300
small intestine	fire	1300-1500
bladder	water	1500-1700
kidney	water	1700-1900
circulation/sex	fire	1900-2100
triple warmer	fire	2100-2300
gall bladder	wood	2300-0100
liver	wood	0100-0300

Heat therapy or moxabustion is sometimes used in conjunction with acupuncture. Acupuncture on its own, as a cold process, is considered yin in nature, and is mainly used to combat illnesses caused by an excess of yang. In moxabustion or *aich'i-u*, pulverized leaves of the mugwort plant are heated and placed on or above the required meridian point after the acupuncture needles have been withdrawn.

Other methods of stimulating ch'i flow through the meridians include:

cupping—placing a cup or glass in which a vacuum has been created by burning herbs or paper in alcohol over the required spot.

blood drawing—the cupping treatment, as above, but as used for snake and poisonous insect bites, with an incision made, and a fairly large amount of blood being drawn from the affected limb or body area.

hot baths and compresses using a variety of herbs, salts, poultices etc.

Shiatsu and acupressure

A healing therapy developed in Japan and known as shiatsu complements acupuncture. It equates with a similar Chinese acupressure healing art known as *tien ch'en*. Shiatsu is based on the use of the same meridian principles as acupuncture, but instead of employing needles, the shiatsu practitioner applies finger pressure to key points on the body to achieve similar results. As we have already learned, martial artists have favored this form of healing for its simplicity, using key points on the body as targets for attack, as well as for the purpose of resuscitation and for the promotion of energy and strength. Pressure applied, for instance, on certain spots on the shoulders and neck will activate a regeneration of fighting spirit, and create the frame of mind required to develop the will to win.

Shiatsu can also be used by anyone to guard against or alleviate the symptoms of colds, stomach, and other bodily disorders, such as headaches, or even hemorrhage, as well as to stimulate sexual capability. Some suggested easy-to-follow acupressure/shiatsu techniques are given below for the reader to try. (If pain or discomfort persists, however, it is expressly suggested that professional medical advice be sought. The authors give no guarantee whatsoever that the methods presented will work in any given case, nor will they accept any liability whatsoever in connection with their use.)

Acupressure therapy for headache:

Method 1: Move the forefinger along a central line on the top of the head, front to back, from the hairline to the crown, searching out tender spots. When a particularly sensitive spot is located, press on it for about 10 seconds, and then move on.

Method 2: Sitting in a chair, apply pressure behind the knees of both legs simultaneously, while holding the head upright to form a triangle. The main pressure should be exerted through the middle fingers.

Method 3: Clasp the arms together by grasping each wrist with the fingers of the other hand, and apply pressure. This method is especially effective when the pain is in the front part of the head.

Acupressure therapy for indigestion and/or stomach pain:

Interlock the fingers of both hands. Place the thumbs on a point about three inches above the navel, and apply pressure for 5 to 10 minutes.

Acupressure therapy for toothache:

Method 1: Place the right index finger on the fleshy part of the left hand, between the thumb and index finger. At the same time, place the left thumb on the same part of the right hand. Exert pressure simultaneously with right index finger and left thumb. Hold this position for 5 to 10 minutes.

Method 2: Place three fingers on the cheek directly above the offending tooth, and apply pressure for 5 to 10 minutes, or until the pain subsides.

Acupressure therapy for sore throat:

Open the mouth and extend the tongue outward, as far as possible. Hold for 20 seconds, then relax, and repeat. (This will bring blood to the throat to initiate self-healing.)

Acupressure therapy for calming the nerves:

Clasp the left thumb tightly in the right hand while holding the right hand with the remaining four fingers of the left. Keep this position for about 5 minutes. (This is a good technique to use to calm the mind prior to meditation.)

Acupressure therapy for skin toning and hormone stimulation:

Bend the neck slightly forward and place the left thumb at the base of the neck (front), about half an inch above the clavicle. Press gently for 2 seconds, repeating five times on the left, and then switching over hands, and repeat the process on the right side of the neck, again five times for 2 seconds each time. Perform the entire series, left and right, three times.

Acupressure therapy for improving sexual performance:

Method 1: Press a point in the pit of the stomach, just below the rib cage, with three fingers. Repeat ten times, for 5 seconds each time.

Method 2: Run the index finger down the lower part of the lumbar region, between the waist and the coccyx, searching out tender spots. When one is located, press lightly ten times for 3 seconds each. In men, this shiatsu exercise will also help control premature ejaculation.

Method 3: Apply pressure with both thumbs simultaneously moving down the jawline, from just below the ears to a point midway to the chin. If any sore spots are located, apply pressure on them for a few seconds before moving on. Repeat three times.

An extension of the shiatsu/tien ch'en acupressure healing techniques involves the stimulation of certain points on the sole of each foot that are linked with the ch'i energy meridians, and, consequently, with specific bodily organs and limbs. This form of therapy has already become especially popular in the West and many books on the subject have become available. Likewise, there are important pressure points on each hand and wrist. Great benefit can be had from an overall massage of the hands (including each finger) and feet (including each toe) as a general body conditioning procedure. A special martial artist's trick for getting the circulation going on waking in the morning is to rub the knee region with a warm hand. This will make the whole leg and foot warm, and is a marvelous counter to poor blood circulation, arthritis, and rheumatism.

12 ☯ Return to the way of peace

> Even when greeted with swords and
> spears it never loses its quiet way.
>
> *Manual of Zen Buddhism*

We have specifically chosen to end this book with a chapter on the use of a weapon of war, the sword, as an instrument of healing, for the symbolism thus invoked expresses for us what we perceive as the true intention behind all martial arts activity.

Although use of various weapons is a prominent feature within the martial arts systems of other countries of the East, Japan is generally accepted as the home of most of the major fighting arts involving use of swords, spears, bows, staffs, and so forth. The classic Japanese weapons schools have existed for many centuries, dedicated to *kendo* (way of the sword), kyudo (way of the bow), *so-jutsu* (art of the spear), and a host of other weapons, such as the *bo* (staff), and the well-known *nunchaku*—a weapon consisting of two lengths of polished wood joined by a metal chain, which has become highly popular in the West.

Japan's oldest, still-surviving weapons academy was established over 500 years ago, in the year 1447, at a location which now lies just a few miles from Tokyo's international airport at Narita. A peep any day through the windows of Tenshin Shoden Katori Shinto Ryu might reveal a couple of individuals doing fierce battle, clad in full, medieval samurai armor, and each armed with sword, staff, or spear—or perhaps halberd, a long-handled weapon of the Middle Ages which consisted of a spear and battle-ax combined. Although the ancient skills learned by the students at this prestigious weapons academy may never be put into ultimate practical application (other than in movie and television epics), total dedication to the chosen art remains the watchword, involving an almost exact duplication of the arts of war as they were seen over five centuries ago.

The founder of the school, Choisai, a former samurai warrior, lived until he was 102 years old. He left a legacy of practical and philosophical teaching which has been faithfully carried forward by a long line of successors.

Method of the peaceful warrior

The essence of Choisai's teaching is revealed in the Japanese word "heiho." Written in Japanese script, heiho means "method of the warrior"; painted in Chinese characters, it means "peaceful." This apparent paradox, as we have already discovered, is strictly in tune with the occult traditions of most bujutsu, or martial arts disciplines— and in the case of what might be termed the most theatrical of the Japanese weapons arts, very much a reflection of the physical truth.

Koji Yada standing before the gateway of a Buddhist shrine.

Kendo—"way of the sword"—was originally known as *ken-jutsu,* or "art of the sword," the samurai method of fencing for combat. In olden times, ken-jutsu was practiced by the samurai warrior with one intention only—to dispatch an opponent swiftly and finally with the *katana,* or two-handed, long sword with a single-edge, curved blade. Until the introduction of the *bokuto* (a sword constructed of heavy red oak wood), the samurai, and the earlier bushi warriors, learned their skill using a live steel blade.

In modern sporting kendo, three types of sword are used. As a *kendoka,* or student of kendo, progresses in skill, he/she will use, in turn, a *shinai,* or bamboo sword, a bokuto (wooden sword) and a katana (a genuine sword of steel). This modern katana sword still duplicates the weapon used by the samurai of old. What is not generally known is that, during the days of the samurai, the katana served a dual purpose—as a weapon of combat, and as an instrument of healing.

Way of bushi

Between the twelfth and nineteenth centuries, the Japanese samurai warrior was perhaps the best known of all fighting men in the East. A certain mystique surrounded samurai martial activities and they were revered for their marvelous combat skills, for their discipline, and for their deep pride in their own stoicism. Known in former times as bushi, the ideal samurai warrior obeyed without question an unwritten code of conduct, or bushido, which held bravery, personal loyalty, and honor above life itself. Under the strict samurai code, the only alternative to defeat or dishonor was considered to be ritual suicide by *seppuku,* or self-disembowelment. The aristocratic samurai warrior culture dominated Japan for over two centuries. When it reached its peak during the Muromachi period (1338 to 1573 C.E.), the samurai constituted a basically rural gentry of considerable influence and power. During this time the influence of Zen Buddhism prompted the introduction to the warrior code of such refinements as poetry, the unique Japanese tea ceremony and the art of flower arranging, all of which continue to this day. The soft and the hard—yin and yang—resided side by side in the samurai's life and these ofttimes violent and murderous characters could frequently be observed sniffing a flower or rhapsodizing over an unusual sunset.

But, perhaps above all else, they were most famous for their ability to use a variety of swords in single combat. The samurai and his ever-present swords could, indeed, be considered synonymous.

In the early 1600s, the Tokugawa Shogun military dictatorship made the samurai, who represented about ten per cent of the population, into a closed caste. This was done to freeze the social order and stabilize control over society. The Shogun era in Japan brought with it a period of some 250 years of peace, but by this time, as a fighting force, the samurai had already become something of an anachronism. The introduction of the musket around the mid-1500s had, to a certain extent, made their prowess with sword, spear, and bow obsolete. The Tokugawa Shoguns were, however, always mindful of the unique advantages contained within the samurai bushido code. A previous role as fighter was now turned into that of administrator. But the days of the true samurai class were numbered, and the samurai's privileged position in

Japanese society was finally taken away when the system of feudalism was abolished in 1871.

Some discontented members of the class displayed the old samurai spirit and rose in rebellion during the 1870s, but the revolts were easily suppressed by the newly formed Japanese army.

Many a samurai now found himself without an effective feudal master, and took on the role of a wandering "sword for hire," the so-called ronin, a name also previously given to renegade samurai warriors with nowhere to go when their domains were confiscated by their *dai-myo,* or feudal lords, during unstable periods in Japan's history. Ronin means literally "wave man," a metaphor for a masterless samurai being carried along without any clear sense of direction, like a wave in the middle of the ocean without a beach on which to roll and crash. Some samurai-turned-ronin became mercenaries and bandits, or turned to the ninja for aid and, as honorable fighting men, joined their ranks. Others began to use, for the benefit of all, the more peaceful of the many samurai skills previously reserved for their own class.

One of these skills was the art of "ki healing," using the katana sword. The katana, which replaced the longer tachi sword when most fighting moved from combat on horseback to combat on foot, has always been regarded by the Japanese as a very precious and symbolic weapon, even invested with the soul of the samurai. The weapon was forged during a long purification ritual process that was considered magickal by the swordsmith and his customer, and each swordmaking master kept his own secret methods to be only handed down from father to son or chosen apprentice. On a strictly practical level, the involved forging operation was always designed to pro-

Koji Yada—The way of the sword.

duce a weapon that would cut well and not break in battle. This end was usually achieved during a complex swordmaking process that started with the production of suitable steel from iron ore. A bar of tool steel was first beaten flat and then repeatedly notched, folded, re-hammered, and hot-forged to produce a final product that consisted of multiple laminations of steel. When the folding and hammering process was repeated around 20 to 30 times, astoundingly, several million layers could eventually result, as has been proved by mathematical calculation. Most swordsmiths incorporated several bars of tool steel, some hard, some soft, and from different sources. Other stages in swordmaking included: quench-hardening by plunging a hot blade into cold water, while making sure that the back of the blade remained soft for extra resilience when used; encasement in specially mixed clay compounds; and, finally, painstaking shaping and polishing.

Return to the way of peace

The most famous of all samurai swordmasters was a dynamic character named Miyamoto Musashi, who was born toward the end of the sixteenth century. Coming from a long line of samurai, and apparently born with the gift of the sword, at the age of thirteen Musashi slew in single combat a famous ken-jutsu master many years his senior. This famous contest established his credentials in most dramatic fashion, and his subsequent exploits were to make him a legend in his own lifetime. He was alleged to have such control over his swordstroke that he was able to split a grain of rice placed on another man's forehead without drawing any blood.

Apart from his stunning prowess as a swordsman, Master Musashi was revered as a man of great culture, despite the fact that he was said to seldom change his clothes or take a bath. He excelled at calligraphy, classical painting, and poetry, and based his life around the art of meditation. At the age of 60, he chose to retire to a cave, to live in piety and to write his classic *Gorin no Sho*, "Essays on the Five Circles" (also published as *A Book of Five Rings* by Overlook Press, New York), which is both a spiritual treatise and a manual of sword tactics. Mushashi's tomb at Kumamoto remains a place of pilgrimage to this day. His fencing technique involving the use of two swords

Koji-Yada—Return to the way of peace.

eventually developed into a ken-jutsu system known as *niten-ichi-ryu*.

Moving into the present time, Koji ("Daido") Yada, now a resident on the Gold Coast of Australia, and who comes originally from the Oita district on Kyushu Island, Japan, was born into a family with a long warrior history stretching back to the days of the samurai. A former Shinto priest, who has also lived for seven years as a Buddhist monk, he is a master of the niten-ichi-ryu combat discipline. Echoing the sentiments of Choisai given earlier in relation to the dual meaning of the word *heiho* (i.e., "peaceful" and "method of the warrior"), and in harmony with the final peaceful retirement of Master Musashi to his meditation cave, Master Koji's father, who fought with the Japanese army during World War II, revealed to his son after the war that he was actually pleased that the terms of the surrender to the Allies now prevented Japan from having a standing army. When he returned home from the fighting, he informed his son: "The warrior may now return at last to the way of peace."

In keeping with his father's desire, and in his honor, Koji Yada has very kindly shared with us some of the healing arts associated with the use of the sword. (Note: This unique method of healing and energizing using ki/ch'i energy will be enlarged upon further in a forthcoming joint work on the healing and magickal rituals of Japan, now in preparation.) The principle involved in ki healing using a sword is an actual transference of ki (ch'i) energy from the healer to the patient via agency of the sword. For the alchemists of old, the sword was a symbol of purifying fire, and magicians would use the sword, or its symbol, for protection against psychic attack. Great heroes of old frequently carried a magical sword, thought to be possessed of great power. Ideally, ki transference and/or healing should be done using a genuine Japanese samurai-type katana sword. However, we have observed that a suitable kitchen or fruit knife will do the job quite adequately, if the necessary sword is not available. The process will not operate, however, if a non-metal energy transmitter is utilized. We have also been told that it is important to have a sharpened edge on the healing instrument.

Ki healing using a sword

Obviously, extreme care should be taken in handling such a sharpened object as a sword or knife (and the authors, of course, can bear no responsibility for their misuse by anyone).

Traditionally, the samurai healer would, when required, hold the blade of his sword with one hand, using a piece of folded rice paper (for the dual purpose of not affecting ki currents and not tarnishing the metal), while keeping it well under control with his other hand held firmly on the hilt.

It is important for the patient to be relaxed at all times, but also totally aware, ready to receive the ki energy, and certainly not in a vague or trance-like state—i.e., not too tense and not too relaxed, but balanced.

The healer should also hold him/herself in a totally balanced state of relaxed awareness.

There are two methods of transferring ki energy by use of a sword or knife: by the point; or by the blade—the sharp, cutting edge is used, with the blade held in one hand (using a piece of folded rice or other paper) and the hilt in the other hand.

The reason for using a piece of paper to hold the blade is so that there is no interference with the flow of ki energy from healer to patient via the sword. A form of a "short circuit" type reaction may occur if an uncovered hand is used.

The points and areas of the body aimed at in ki/sword healing are generally the same meridian points as used in acupuncture and/or shiatsu. There is also a series of eight special healing areas—each associated with a specific set of organs, complaints, etc.—which can be linked with the seven chakras or energy vortice of the Indian yoga system. These are located as follows:

1. Crown of the head: clearing the mind; treatment of neuroses and mental complaints. (Note: see also item 8 below.)

2. Central forehead ("third eye"): headaches; eye and nose problems; enhancement of mental concentration.

3. Throat area: hormone balancing; throat and lung problems; to create calming and and/or soothing effect.

4. Heart area: cardiac problems; regulation of heart beat—either up or down; general relaxation.

5. Solar plexus: stomach/digestive disorders; liver, pancreas and spleen ailments; nerve stimulation; also some heart conditions.

6. Navel: general body toning.

7. Hara (three fingers below navel): stimulation of vital energy; transfer of ki (ch'i) from one person to another.

8. Base of spine: sexual organ disorders; anal complaints (i.e. hemorrhoids). (Note: see also 1 above.)

Special notes

For any kidney function complaints, the ki entry spot is placed between the third and fourth lumbar vertebrae of the spine.

For ailments detailed under 1 and 8, both points should be stimulated in each case as the crown point and base of spine point complete an "energy circuit."

The kiai shout

Essential to the transfer of ki energy from healer to patient is use of the kiai "shout of power." Kiai, as we have already learned (Chapter 3), means something like "spirit meeting" and is the violent exhalation of air, in the form of a shout, used in karate and other martial arts disciplines. Originating in the diaphragm, it is forced up to the throat by the muscles of the lower abdomen, the area of the body which is thought to be the source of all power—the ki/ch'i hara energy point, about three fingers below the navel.

When used in healing and energy transference, the kiai sounding should be quite drawn out, starting deep down in the abdomen, almost like a low growl, and increasing in intensity and rising in pitch as it is forced up the throat and out of the mouth, ending on a high-pitched note.

The pronunciation of the shout as taught us by Master Koji is exactly as per the syllables contained in its descriptive name, but drawn out during the raising of ki energy from the healer's hara, up through the body and arms, and via the sword to the patient: *kkkiiiiiiiiiiii—ai*, starting with a low almost growling sound, shifting up in pitch all the time, and with a very strong emphasis on the final high-pitched *ai*.

Therapy procedures

The following general procedures are recommended, but can be varied to suit any particular individual case.

Note that there are two distinct methods of passing ki energy from healer to patient—one using the kiai shout (for energizing) and one in silence (for calming and relaxation).

First series: the seiza position

The patient can either be seated sideways in a chair or, preferably, be placed in the traditional on-the-knees Japanese seiza, or sitting position, with feet tucked up under the buttocks (see Chapter 10 for description). If the seiza position is used, remember that the patient's hands should rest lightly on his/her knees and that, for a man, the knees should be two clenched fists apart, and for a woman, one clenched fist apart. In the seiza position or on a chair, the patient's shoulders should be relaxed and down, with back straight, head erect (as if there were a plumb line entering at the crown), and eyes looking straight ahead. Also, in either case, it is desirable for the patient's big toes to be touching, one resting atop the other, in order to close the body's energy circuit.

(a) Pre-treatment relaxation: Holding the sword/knife firmly by the hilt with one hand, take the blade in the other hand using a folded piece of clean white paper to hold it. Place the cutting edge of the blade gently on the middle part of the patient's shoulder, and start a gentle rocking motion while balancing the sword/knife between the two hands, without applying any pressure at all, and while causing no discomfort to the patient. This action should lead to a general feeling of better relaxation and can also be used to bring down the inflammation in very tense or injured muscles. (Do each shoulder in turn and do not use the kiai shout.)

(b) Crown of the head: Again holding the sword/knife in two hands, with one hand on the hilt and the other holding the point of the blade using a piece of paper, place the center of the flat of the blade very gently on the crown of the patient's head. Remember, there must be no added pressure, only the weight of the sword/knife itself. Hold the sword/knife completely still, with both hands, and transfer ki energy from healer to patient through use of the kiai shout as described above. While sounding the kiai, the healer is to concentrate on raising the ki energy from his/her own hara energy, carried upwards by the kiai breath, through the arms, and thence to the patient via the sword/knife. Both healer and patient must remain relaxed but alert.

Now, again grasping the hilt in one hand, and the blade in the other, near but not quite at the point, again using a sheet of folded paper, place the point of the sword/knife on the mid-crown position (use the blade in a flat position). Hold for a moment, and use the kiai technique as described in (a) to transfer ki energy to the patient.

(This treatment might, in some ways, be related to electrical shock therapy.) Important note: When invoking the healing ki energy through use of the kiai shout, keep the sword/knife transmitter perfectly still and steady at all times.

(c) Central forehead/third eye: Same as above, but using sword/knife point only (not in a "flat" position as before).

(d) Throat area: Again, use point only, but repeat on either side of the throat area.

(e) Heart area: Use point only.

(f) Solar plexus: Use point only.

(g) Navel: Use point only.

(h) Hara (three fingers below navel): Use point only.

(i) Base of spine: Use point only.

(j) 3/4 lumbar point (for kidney complaints): Use point only.

Second series: lying down

Lay the patient down on his/her back and use the "blade of the sword" methods only, as described in (a) and (b) above, for relaxation and transference of ki energy purposes to the heart, solar plexus, navel and hara areas only. Do not use this position for any healing work on the head or throat, and note never to use the point of the sword/knife when the patient is lying down. For work on the base of the spine and lumbar point regions, have the patient turn over, face down— but again, do not use the point of the sword/knife when a patient is in any lying-down position.

Closing and cleansing

At the close of any healing session, the healer should mentally place a circle of white light protection around the patient; if desired, a cross enclosed in a circle can be made with the sword/knife or empty hand, in front and back of the patient.

It is also very important to thoroughly cleanse the sword/knife under running water after use, so as not to transfer energy vibrations from one patient to the next. This can best be accomplished employing a method used by some magicians involving a visualization process: Holding the blade of the sword/knife under running water, gather ki energy from the hara into the solar plexus area, and then project it through the hand or hands holding the sword/knife as a "blue light." Visualize this blue light sweeping all impurities out of the blade into the running water.

As an alternative closing and protection ritual, a magickal circle of protection can be drawn around the patient by projecting the blue light from the point of the extended blade while completing the circular movement.

Glossary of important terms

acupuncture—Chinese healing art involving the placement of thin, sharp needles in the body at special "meridian points in order to facilitate healing

aikido—Way of fundamental, or divine, harmony or Way of harmony with universal energy

atemi—application of pressure on certain vulnerable points on the body

Ch'an—Zen

chang chuan (see chung-kuo chuan)

ch'i—primal energy

ch'i-k'ung—the art of using ch'i force

ch'i-li nung—ch'i control

chung-kuo chuan (also chang chuan)—Chinese fist or hand

dim muk—touch of death

dojo—training hall

feng shui—literally "wind/water"; Chinese earth magick

hapkido—art of coordinated power

hara—ch'i or ki center

hsia chen pien—acupuncture

hsing-i—the will

hwrang-do—way of the flowering manhood

jeet kune-do—way of the intercepting fist

jing—organic life-form essence

judo—the gentle way

ju-jutsu—way of flexibility

karate—empty hand China hand

katana—two-handed long sword with a single-edge curved blade

kendo—way of the sword

ken-jutsu—art of the sword

ketsu-in—see mudra ki (see ch'i)

kiai—karate shout of power (literally: spirit meeting)

k'ung fu—hard work by someone at a special skill (fu = man; k'ung = power or force)

kime—coordinated energy forces of the body, mind, and spirit

kokyu—level of ability in use of ki/ch'i energy

kuatsu—an ancient method of resuscitation

kyudo—art of the bow/way of the bow

kyokushinkai—style of the ultimate truth

l'i—higher life force; immutable law of the universe

Lohan-k'ung—see shih-pa Lo Han sho

mudra (Japan: ketsu-in)—placing of the fingers of the hand in certain positions in order to channel and direct essential energy

ninjutsu—art of the ninja

nui-k'ung—inner power

seika-no-itten—vital point of ki center

seiza—Japanese formal style of sitting

Shaolin chuan—Shaolin fist

shiatsu—finger pressure healing

shih-pa Lo Han sho (also Lohan-k'ung)—eighteen hands of the Lo Han

shindai—bed or pillow fighting

Shinto—Way of the gods

shorinji kempo—Shaolin temple fist way

so—the mathematical principle behind all creation

so-jutsu—art of the spear

sui so do—way of secret magick

taekwon-do—way of the foot and fist

t'ai ch'i chuan—grand ultimate fist

tang soo do—way of the knife

tien che'n—acupressure

Wu ch'i—unnameable emptiness from which all creation springs

wu shu—war arts

yabusame—archery on horseback

yang—positive aspect of the universe (fullness, the sun, hardness, male, mobility, etc.)

yin—negative aspect of the universe (softness, night, female, the moon, immobility, etc.)

ying-ch'i-k'ung—practitioner of chi'i-k'ung

Bibliography

Anton, Jacques and St. Denise, Claude. *Bruce Lee's "My Martial Arts Training Manual."* New York, NY: Zebra Books, 1976.

Australasian Fighting Arts (magazine). Manly, NSW, Australia: Australasian Martial Arts Publishers Pty Ltd., various issues.

Barclay, Glen. *Mind Over Matter.* London: Pan Books, 1973.

Black Belt (magazine). Burbank, CA: Rainbow Publications, Inc., various issues.

Blitz Martial Arts Magazine. Geelong, Australia: Blitz Publishers, various issues.

Camphausen, Rufus C. *The Divine Library.* Rochester, Vermont: Inner Traditions International, Ltd., 1992.

Capra, Fritjof. *The Tao of Physics.* Boulder, CO: Shambhala Publications, 1976.

Carlile, Richard. *Manual of Freemasonry.* London: William Reeves, no date.

Carradine, David. *Spirit of Shaolin.* Sydney: Random House Australia, 1991.

Cavendish, Richard. *A History of Magic.* London: Weidenfeld and Nicolson, 1977.

Chee Soo. *The Taoist Ways of Healing*. Wellingborough, Northants: The Aquarian Press, 1986.

Choy, Howard. *Lohan Kung*. Sidney: Choy Lee Fut Martial Arts Federation, 1984.

Chung-liang Huang, Al. *Embrace Tiger, Return to Mountain*. Moab, Utah: Real People Press, 1973.

Ch'u Ta-Kao. *Tao Te Ching*. London: Buddhist Lodge, 1937.

Conway, David. *Magic: An Occult Primer*. Wellingborough, Northants: The Aquarian Press, 1988.

Crowley, Brian & Esther. *Understanding the Oriental Martial Arts*. Sydney: RBC, 1987.

Crowley, Brian & Esther. *Words of Power*. St. Paul, MN: Llewellyn, 1991.

Da Liu. *The Tao of Health and Longevity*. London: Routledge and Kegan Paul, 1979.

Douglas, Alfred. *The Oracle of Change—How to Consult the I Ching*. London: Penquin Books, 1972.

Eisenberg, David & Wright, Thomas. *Encounters with Qi: Exploring Chinese Medicine*. London: Jonathan Cape, 1986.

Eliade, Mircea. *Shamanism: Archaic Techniques of Ecstasy*. Princeton: Pollingen Foundation, 1974.

Fighting Stars Ninja (magazine). Burbank, CA: Rainbow Publications, Inc., various issues.

Finn, Michael. *The Martial Arts: A Complete Illustrated History*. New York: The Overlook Press, 1988.

Gleeson, Geoff. *The Complete Book of Judo*. Toronto: Coles, 1976.

Harrison, E. J. *The Fighting Spirit of Japan.* New York: Foulsham, 1960.

Hatsumi, Dr. M. *Ninjutsu History and Tradition.* Hollywood, CA: Unique Publications, 1981.

Hayes, Stephen K. *Ninjutsu: The Art of the Invisible Warrior.* Chicago: Contemporary Books, Inc., 1984.

————. *The Mystic Arts of the Ninja.* Chicago: Contemporary Books, Inc., 1985.

Holbrook, Bruce. *The Stone Monkey: An Alternative Chinese-Scientific Reality.* New York: William Morrow and Company, Inc., 1981.

Horwitz, Ted and Kimmelman, Susan with Lui, H. H. *Tai Chi Chu'an: The Technique of Power.* London: Rider, 1979.

Huai-Chin Nan (trans. Wen Kuan Chu). *Tao and Longevity.* Longmead, Dorset: Element Books, 1984.

Hyams, Joe. *Zen in the Martial Arts.* New York: Bantam Books, 1982.

Inside Karate (magazine). Burbank, CA: CFW Enterprises, Inc., various issues.

Inside Kung Fu (magazine). Burbank, CA: CFW Enterprises, Inc., various issues.

Karate Illustrated (magazine). Burbank, CA: Rainbow Publications, Inc., various issues.

Kent, Graeme. *Fighting Sports.* London: Macmillan, 1981.

Kubota, Shihan Tak. *The Art of Karate.* New York: Peebles Press, 1977.

Lagerwey, John. *Taoist Ritual in Chinese Society and History.* New York: Macmillan Publishing Company, 1987.

Lewis, Peter. *Martial Arts of the Orient*. Sydney: Golden Press, 1985.

_____. *The Way to the Martial Arts*. Sydney: Golden Press, 1986.

Ludzia, Leo F. *Life Force*. St. Paul, MN: Llewellyn, 1989.

Mitchell, David. *Official Karate*. London: Stanley Paul, 1986.

Mutwa, Vusamazulu Credo. *Indaba My Children*. Johannesburg: Blue Crane Books, 1967.

Namikoshi, Tokujiro. *Shiatsu: Japanese Finger-Pressure Therapy*. Tokyo: Japan Publications, 1969.

Official Karate (magazine). Derby, CN: Charlton Publications, Inc., various issues.

Oyama, Masutatsu. *This is Karate*. Los Angeles: Martial Arts, 1964.

Page, Michael. *The Power of Ch'i*. Wellingborough, Northants: The Aquarian Press, 1988.

Pang Jen Lo, Benjamin; Inn, Martin; Amacher, Robert; and Foe, Susan. *The Essence of T'ai Chi Ch'uan*. Berkley, CA: North Atlantic Books, 1985.

Parulski, George R. *The Art of Karate Weapons*. Chicago: Contemporary Books, Inc., 1984.

Payne, Peter. *Martial Arts: The Spiritual Dimension*. London: Thames and Hudson, 1981.

Pearson, Carol S. *The Hero Within: Six Archetypes for the Way We Live*. San Francisco: Harper & Row, 1989.

Peterson, Kirtland C. *Mind of the Ninja: Exploring the Inner Power*. Chicago: Contemporary Books, Inc., 1986.

Picken, Stuart D. B. *Shinto—Japan's Spiritual Roots*. Tokyo: Kodansha International, 1980.

Pike, Geoff. *The Power of Ch'i.* Sidney: Bay Books, Ltd., 1980.

Random, Michael. *The Martial Arts.* London: Peerage Books, 1984.

Rawson, Philip and Legeza, Laszlo. *Tao: The Chinese Philosophy of Time and Change.* London: Thames and Hudson, 1973.

Reid, Howard & Croucher, Michael. *The Way of the Warrior.* London: Century Publishing, 1983.

Reps, Paul. *Zen Flesh, Zen Bones, A Collection of Zen and Pre-Zen Writings.* London: M. Paterson & Co., 1959.

Ross, Nancy Wilson. *Three Ways of Asian Wisdom: Hinduism, Buddhism and Zen.* London: Faber & Faber, 1966.

Schumaker, Ellen and Nobunuga, Tomi. *Shindai: The Art of Japanese Bed-Fighting.* London: Wolfe Publishing, Ltd., 1965.

Shapiro, Amy. *The Language of the Martial Arts.* London: W. H. Allen, 1981.

Suzuki, Daisetz Eitaro. *A Manual of Zen Buddhism.* Kyoto: Eastern Buddhist Society, 1935.

_____. *Introduction to Zen Buddhism* including "A manual of Zen Buddhism." New York: Causeway Books, 1973.

Taekwondo (magazine). Davenport, IA: Tri-Mount Publications, various issues.

Tohei, Koichi. *Aikido in Daily Life.* Tokyo: Rikugel Publishing House, 1966.

Turnbull, Stephen R. *The Book of the Samurai.* London: Bison Books, 1982.

Ueshiba, Kisshomaru. *The Spirit of Aikido.* Tokyo: Kodansha International, 1984.

Veith, Ilza (translator). *The Yellow Emperor's Classic of Internal Medicine.* Berkeley, CA: University of California Press, 1966.

Warriors (magazine). New York: Condor Books, Inc., various issues.

Watts, Alan W. *The Spirit of Zen.* New York: Grove Press, Inc., 1960.

Webster-Doyle, Terrence. *Karate: The Art of Empty Self.* Berkley, CA: North Atlantic Books, 1986.

Wilhelm, Richard (trans.). *The Secret of the Golden Flower: A Chinese Book of Life.* New York: Harvest Books, 1970.

Williams, Bryn (ed.). *Martial Arts of the Orient.* London: Hamlyn, 1975.

Yamasaki, Taiko. *Shingon: Japanese Esoteric Buddhism.* Boston: Shambhala Publications, 1988.

Yiu, Tennyson. *Tai Chi.* Sidney: Garry Burke, Jack Thompson, Tennyson Yiu, 1984.

Yutang, Lin. *The Importance of Living.* London: Heinemann, 1938.

STAY IN TOUCH

On the following pages you will find some of the books now available on related subjects. Your book dealer stocks most of these and will stock new titles in the Llewellyn series as they become available. We urge your patronage.

To obtain our full catalog, to keep informed about new titles as they are released and to benefit from informative articles and helpful news, you are invited to write for our bimonthly news magazine/catalog, *Llewellyn's New Worlds of Mind and Spirit*. A sample copy is free, and it will continue coming to you at no cost as long as you are an active mail customer. Or you may subscribe for just $10.00 in the U.S.A. and Canada ($20.00 overseas, first class mail). Many bookstores also have *New Worlds* available to their customers. Ask for it.

Llewellyn's New Worlds of Mind and Spirit
P.O. Box 64383-134, St. Paul, MN 55164-0383, U.S.A.

* * *

TO ORDER BOOKS AND TAPES

If your book dealer does not have the books described, you may order them directly from the publisher by sending full price in U.S. funds, plus $3.00 for postage and handling for orders *under* $10.00; $4.00 for orders *over* $10.00. There are no postage and handling charges for orders over $50.00. Postage and handling rates are subject to change. We ship UPS whenever possible. Delivery guaranteed. Provide your street address as UPS does not deliver to P.O. Boxes. UPS to Canada requires a $50.00 minimum order. Allow 4-6 weeks for delivery. Orders outside the U.S.A. and Canada: Airmail—add retail price of book; add $5.00 for each non-book item (tapes, etc.); add $1.00 per item for surface mail.

FOR GROUP STUDY AND PURCHASE

Because there is a great deal of interest in group discussion and study of the subject matter of this book, we offer a special quantity price to group leaders or agents. Our special quantity price for a minimum order of five copies of *Moving with the Wind* is $30.00 cash-with-order. This price includes postage and handling within the United States. Minnesota residents must add 6.5% sales tax. For additional quantities, please order in multiples of five. For Canadian and foreign orders, add postage and handling charges as above. Credit card (VISA, MasterCard, American Express) orders are accepted. Charge card orders only ($15.00 minimum order) may be phoned in free within the U.S.A. or Canada by dialing 1-800-THE-MOON. For customer service, call 1-612-291-1970. Mail orders to:

LLEWELLYN PUBLICATIONS
P.O. Box 64383-134, St. Paul, MN 55164-0383, U.S.A.

Prices subject to change without notice.

**16 STEPS TO HEALTH AND ENERGY: A Program of Color &
Visual Meditation, Movement & Chakra Balance
by Pauline Wills & Theo. Gimble**
Before an illness reaches your physical body, it has already been in
your auric body for days, weeks, even months. By the time you feel
sick, something in your life has been out of balance for a while. But
why wait to get sick to get healthy? Follow the step-by-step techniques
in *16 Steps to Health and Energy,* and you will open up the energy cir-
cuits of your subtle body so you are better able to stay balanced and
vital in our highly toxic and stressful world.

Our subtle anatomy includes the "energy" body of seven chakras that
radiate the seven colors of the spectrum. Each chakra responds well to
a particular combination of yoga postures and color visualizations, all
of which are provided in this book.

At the end of the book is a series of 16 "workshops" that help you to
travel through progressive stages of consciousness expansion and self-
transformation. Each session deals with a particular color and all of its
associated meditations, visualizations, and yoga postures. Here is a
truly holistic route to health at all levels! Includes 16 color plates!
0-87542-871-1, 224 pgs., 6 x 9, illus., softcover $12.95

**CHAKRA THERAPY
For Personal Growth & Healing
by Keith Sherwood**
Understand yourself, know how your body and mind function and
learn how to overcome negative programming so that you can become
a free, healthy, self-fulfilled human being.

This book fills in the missing pieces of the human anatomy system left
out by orthodox psychological models. It serves as a superb work-
book. Within its pages are exercises and techniques designed to
increase your level of energy, to transmute unhealthy frequencies of
energy into healthy ones, to bring you back into balance and harmony
with your self, your loved ones, and the multidimensional world you
live in. Finally, it will help bring you back into union with the universal field of energy and consciousness.

Chakra Therapy will teach you how to heal yourself by healing your
energy system because it is actually energy in its myriad forms which
determines a person's physical health, emotional health, mental
health, and level of consciousness.
0-87542-721-9, 256 pgs., 5 1/4 x 8, illus., softcover $7.95

ECSTASY THROUGH TANTRA
by Dr. Jonn Mumford
Dr. Jonn Mumford makes the occult dimension of the sexual dynamic accessible to everyone. One need not go up to the mountaintop to commune with Divinity: its temple is the body, its sacrament the communion between lovers. *Ecstasy Through Tantra* traces the ancient practices of sex magick through the Egyptian, Greek, and Hebrew forms, where the sexual act is viewed as symbolic of the highest union, to the highest expression of Western sex magick.

Dr. Mumford guides the reader through mental and physical exercises aimed at developing psychosexual power; he details the various sexual practices and positions that facilitate "psychic short-circuiting" and the arousal of Kundalini, the Goddess of Life within the body. He shows the fundamental unity of Tantra with Western Wicca, and he plumbs the depths of Western sex magick, showing how its techniques culminate in spiritual illumination. Includes 14 full-color photographs.
0-87542-494-5, 190 pgs., 6 x 9, illus., softcover **$12.95**

THE JOY OF HEALTH
A Doctor's Guide to Nutrition and Alternative Medicine
by Zoltan P. Rona M.D., M.Sc.
Finally, a medical doctor objectively explores the benefits and pitfalls of alternative health care, based on exceptional nutritional scholarship, long clinical practice, and wide-ranging interactions with "established" and alternative practitioners throughout North America.

The Joy of Health is must reading before you seek the advice of an alternative health care provider. Can a chiropractor or naturopath help your condition? What are viable alternatives to standard cancer care? Is Candida a real disease? Can you really extend your life with megavitamins? Might hidden food allergies be the root of many physical and emotional problems?

- Get clear-cut answers to the most commonly asked questions about nutrition and preventive medicine
- Explore various treatments for 47 conditions and diseases
- Make informed choices about food, diets and supplements
- Discover startling information about food allergies and related conditions
- Explore 20 different types of diets and recipes
- Cut through advertising claims and vested-interest scare tactics
- Empower yourself to achieve a high level of wellness

0-87542-684-0, 264 pgs., 6 x 9, softcover **$12.95**

Prices subject to change without notice.

THE COMPLETE HANDBOOK OF NATURAL HEALING
by Marcia Starck

Got an itch that won't go away? Want a massage but don't know the difference between Rolfing, Reichian Therapy and Reflexology? Tired of going to the family doctor for minor illnesses that you know you could treat at home—if you just knew how?

Designed to function as a home reference guide (yet enjoyable and interesting enough to be read straight through), this book addresses all natural healing modalities in use today: dietary regimes, nutritional supplements, cleansing and detoxification, vitamins and minerals, herbology, homeopathic medicine and cell salts, traditional Chinese medicine, Ayurvedic medicine, body work therapies, exercise, mental and spiritual therapies, and more. In addition, a section of 41 specific ailments outlines natural treatments for everything from acne to varicose veins.

0-87542-742-1, 416 pgs., 6 x 9 , softcover **$12.95**

HOW TO HEAL WITH COLOR
by Ted Andrews

Now, for perhaps the first time, color therapy is placed within the grasp of the average individual. Anyone can learn to facilitate and accelerate the healing process on all levels with the simple color therapies in *How to Heal with Color*.

Color serves as a vibrational remedy that interacts with the human energy system to stabilize physical, emotional, mental and spiritual conditions. When there is balance, we can more effectively rid ourselves of toxins, negativities and patterns that hinder our life processes.

This book provides color application guidelines that are beneficial for over 50 physical conditions and a wide variety of emotional and mental conditions. Receive simple and tangible instructions for performing "muscle testing" on yourself and others to find the most beneficial colors. Learn how to apply color therapy through touch, projection, breathing, cloth, water and candles. Learn how to use the little known but powerful color-healing system of the mystical Qabala to balance and open the psychic centers. Plus, discover simple techniques for performing long-distance healings on others.

0-87542-005-2, 240 pgs., mass market, illus. **$3.95**

KUNDALINI AND THE CHAKRAS
A Practical Manual—Evolution in this Lifetime
by Genevieve Lewis Paulson

The mysteries of Kundalini revealed! We all possess the powerful evolutionary force of Kundalini that can open us to genius states, psychic powers and cosmic consciousness. As the energies of the Aquarian Age intensify, more and more people are experiencing the "big release" spontaneously but have been ill-equipped to channel its force in a productive manner. This book shows you how to release Kundalini gradually and safely and is your guide to sating the strange, new appetites which result when life-in-process "blows open" your body's many energy centers.

The section on chakras brings new understanding to these "dials" on our life machine (body). It is the most comprehensive information available for cleansing and developing the chakras and their energies. Read *Kundalini and the Chakras* and prepare to make a quantum leap in your spiritual growth!

0-87542-592-5, 224 pgs. 6 x 9, illus., color plates, softcover $12.95

THE WOMEN'S BOOK OF HEALING
by Diane Stein

At the front of the women's spirituality movement with her previous books, Diane Stein now helps women (and men) reclaim their natural right to be healers. Included are exercises which can help YOU to become a healer! Learn about the uses of color, vibration, crystals and gems for healing. Learn about the auric energy field and the chakras.

The book teaches alternative healing theory and techniques and combines them with crystal and gemstone healing, laying on of stones, psychic healing, laying on of hands, chakra work and aura work, and color therapy. It teaches beginning theory in the aura, chakras, colors, creative visualization, meditation, health theory, and ethics, with some quantum theory. Forty-six gemstones plus clear quartz crystals are discussed in detail, arranged by chakras and colors.

The Women's Book of Healing is a book designed to teach basic healing (Part I) and healing with crystals and gemstones (Part II). Part I discusses the aura and four bodies; the chakras; basic healing skills of creative visualization, meditation and color work; psychic healing; and laying on of hands. Part II begins with a chapter on clear quartz crystal, then enters gemstone work with introductory gemstone material. The remainder of the book discusses, in chakra-by-chakra format, specific gemstones for healing work, their properties and uses.

0-87542-759-6, 352 pgs., 6 x 9, illus., softcover $12.95

Prices subject to change without notice.

JUDE'S HERBAL HOME REMEDIES
Natural Health, Beauty & Home-Care Secrets
by Jude C. Williams, M.H.

There's a pharmacy—in your spice cabinet! In the course of daily life we all encounter problems that can be easily remedied through the use of common herbs—headaches, dandruff, insomnia, colds, muscle aches, burns—and a host of other afflictions known to humankind. *Jude's Herbal Home Remedies* is a simple guide to self care that will benefit beginning or experienced herbalists with its wealth of practical advice. Most of the herbs listed are easy to obtain.

Discover how cayenne pepper promotes hair growth, why cranberry juice is a good treatment for asthma attacks, how to make a potent juice to flush out fat, how to make your own deodorants and perfumes, what herbs will get fleas off your pet, how to keep cut flowers fresh longer . . . the remedies and hints go on and on!

This book gives you instructions for teas, salves, tinctures, tonics, poultices, along with addresses for obtaining the herbs. Dangerous and controversial herbs are also discussed.

Grab this book and a cup of herbal tea, and discover from a Master Herbalist more than 800 ways to a simpler, more natural way of life.
0-87542-869-X, 240 pgs., 6 x 9, illus., softcover **$9.95**

RECLAIMING THE POWER
The How & Why of Practical Ritual Magic
by Lady Sabrina

By far one of the most usable and workable approaches to magic written in a long time, *Reclaiming the Power* is for anyone who has ever wondered about magic, ever wanted to try it, or ever had a goal to achieve. This is the first book to explain just what ritual magic is, without the trappings of a specific tradition. It is a simple, straightforward approach to magic, stressing the use of natural and seasonal energies to accomplish what needs to be done.

Getting results is what *Reclaiming the Power* is all about. The average person, untrained and uninitiated, will learn basic magic that can be performed anywhere and for any purpose. They will learn to develop individual power, and use that power through structured rituals to get whatever it is they need or want.

Everything, from what magic is to spell-casting, is explained in simple, easy-to-understand language. All of the rituals presented are complete and can be easily adapted to solitary working.
0-87542-166-0, 256 pgs., 5 1/4 x 8, illus., softcover **$9.95**

Prices subject to change without notice.

TAMING THE DIET DRAGON
Using Language & Imagery for Weight Control
& Body Transformation
by Constance C. Kirk

Do you find dieting a struggle? Do you feel deprived, frustrated and hopeless in your failed attempts to reach and maintain your ideal image? The dismally low success rate of only 5 percent for losing fat and maintaining ideal weight is not because the traditional approaches of diet and exercise do not work. It is because the dieter fails to act in consistently positive ways.

This book is about doing something different. *Taming the Diet Dragon* teaches how to end the struggle and pain of diet and exercise, and successfully lose weight and keep it off. It's about changing the way you think, which in turn changes the way you behave, and even changes your physiology and metabolism! It ultimately is about creating your own reality and fulfilling your best potential.

How do you tame the diet dragon? First through imagery, the quickest way to affect perception and physiology. Secondly through language, necessary to effect long-term changes in attitude, faith and belief. And thirdly through experiential skills, useful in focusing on awareness which is beyond words or images.

0-87542-372-8, 176 pgs., 5 1/4 x 8, softcover $9.95

WORDS OF POWER
Sacred Sounds of East and West
by Brian & Esther Crowley

Tune in . . . to the hidden "sounds of the soul." Within our human heritage is a vast storehouse of magical words, mantras, invocations and chants handed down from ages past. The ancients used these sacred sounds to still the mind, heal the body, and attain higher states of consciousness. These sounds are their gift to us, and they are revealed at last in this fascinating and instantly usable manual.

Words of Power is the first such work of a universal nature, with a selection of potent sounds in Egyptian, Hebrew, Sanskrit, Tibetan, Arabic, Greek, Latin, English, and others. Presented in an easy-to-learn format, *Words of Power* contains simple keys to correct pronunciation, suggested meditations, and detailed explanations of esoteric meanings and functions. This book also explores the origin of the first mantra, the many names of Allah, the important sacred phrase common to all ancient cultures, the meanings of the words of power used by Jesus, and how Moses may have used words of power to part the Red Sea.

0-87542-135-0, 336 pgs., 5 1/4 x 8, illus., softcover $10.95

ENERGIZE!
The Alchemy of Breath & Movement for Health & Transformation
by Elrond, Juliana and Sophia Blawyn and Suzanne Jones

Meeting the needs of our daily obligations can drain us, frustrate us, and slowly kill us in both body and spirit. If you wish to pursue spiritual growth and you lack the strength to devote to this goal, this book can help. With just a few minutes a day of dynamic movement and consciously controlled breathing, you will begin to move your Chi, or vital energy, and you will experience heightened levels of physical energy, greater mental clarity, and a more fit and flexible body. As your reservoir of energy increases, your joy in life will increase, you will possess a greater capacity to function happily and productively in your daily life, and your spiritual progress begins.

Energize! blends the esoteric traditions of yoga, sufism and taoism. You have the remarkable opportunity to learn Chinese *T'ai Chi Chi Kung, T'ai Chi Ruler,* and Red Dragon *Chi Kung;* East Indian Chakra Energizers; Middle Eastern Sufi Earth Dancing, Veil Dancing and Whirling; and the Native American Dance of the Four Directions, all at your own pace in the privacy of your own home.

0-87542-060-5, 240 pgs., 6 x 9, 96 illus., softcover $10.00

THE LLEWELLYN PRACTICAL GUIDE
TO PSYCHIC SELF-DEFENSE AND WELL-BEING
by Denning & Phillips

Psychic well-being and psychic self-defense are two sides of the same coin, just as are physical health and resistance to disease. Each person (and every living thing) is surrounded by an electromagnetic force field, or AURA, that can provide the means to psychic self-defense and to dynamic well-being. This book explores the world of very real "psychic warfare" of which we are all victims. Every person in our modern world is subjected to psychic stress and psychological bombardment: advertising promotions that play upon primitive emotions, political and religious appeals that work on feelings of insecurity and guilt, noise, threats of violence and war, news of crime and disaster, etc.

This book shows the nature of genuine psychic attacks—ranging from actual acts of black magic to bitter jealousy and hate—and the reality of psychic stress, the structure of the psyche and its interrelationship with the physical body. It shows how each person must develop his weakened aura into a powerful defense-shield, thereby gaining both physical protection and energetic well-being that can extend to protection from physical violence, accidents ... even ill health.

0-87542-190-3, 306 pgs., 5 1/4 x 8, illus., softcover $8.95

THE ART OF SPIRITUAL HEALING
by Keith Sherwood

Each of you has the potential to be a healer; to heal yourself and to become a channel for healing others. Healing energy is always flowing through you. Learn how to recognize and tap this incredible energy source. You do not need to be a victim of disease or poor health. Rid yourself of negativity and become a channel for positive healing.

Become acquainted with your three auras and learn how to recognize problems and heal them on a higher level before they become manifested in the physical body as disease.

Special techniques make this book a "breakthrough" to healing power, but you are also given a concise, easy-to-follow regimen of good health to follow in order to maintain a superior state of being. This is a practical guide to healing.

0-87542-720-0, 256 pgs., 5-1/4 x 8, illus., softcover **$7.95**

WHEELS OF LIFE
A User's Guide to the Chakra System
by Anodea Judith

An instruction manual for owning and operating the inner gears that run the machinery of our lives. Written in a practical, down-to-earth style, this fully illustrated book will take the reader on a journey through aspects of consciousness, from the bodily instincts of survival to the processing of deep thoughts.

Discover this ancient metaphysical system under the new light of popular Western metaphors: quantum physics, elemental magick, Kabbalah, physical exercises, poetic meditations, and visionary art. Learn how to open these centers in yourself, and see how the chakras shed light on the present world crises we face today. And learn what you can do about it!

This book will be a vital resource for: Magicians, Witches, Pagans, Mystics, Yoga Practitioners, Martial Arts people, Psychologists, Medical people, and all those who are concerned with holistic growth techniques. The modern picture of the chakras was introduced to the West largely in the context of Hatha and Kundalini Yoga and through the Theosophical writings of Leadbeater and Besant. But the chakra system is equally innate to Western Magick: all psychic development, spiritual growth, and practical attainment is fully dependent upon the opening of the chakras!

0-87542-320-5, 544 pgs., 6 x 9, illus., softcover **$14.95**

THE LLEWELLYN ANNUALS

Llewellyn's MOON SIGN BOOK: Approximately 400 pages of valuable information on gardening, fishing, weather, stock market forecasts, personal horoscopes, good planting dates, and general instructions for finding the best date to do just about anything! Articles by prominent forecasters and writers in the fields of gardening, astrology, politics, economics and cycles. This special almanac, different from any other, has been published annually since 1906. It's fun, informative, and has been a great help to millions in their daily planning.   **State year $4.95**

Llewellyn's SUN SIGN BOOK: Your personal horoscope for the entire year! All 12 signs are included in one handy book. Also included are forecasts, special feature articles, and an action guide for each sign, monthly horoscopes by Gloria Star, author of *Optimum Child*, for your personal Sun Sign, and articles on a variety of subjects by well-known astrologers from around the country. Much more than just a horoscope guide! Entertaining and fun the year around.   **State year $4.95**

Llewellyn's DAILY PLANETARY GUIDE: Includes all of the major daily aspects plus their exact times in Eastern and Pacific time zones, lunar phases, signs and voids plus their times, planetary motion, a monthly ephemeris, sunrise and sunset tables, special articles on the planets, signs, aspects, a business guide, planetary hours, rulerships, and much more. Large 5-1/4 x 8 format for more writing space, spiral bound to lay flat, address and phone listings, time-zone conversion chart and blank horoscope chart.   **State year $6.95**

Llewellyn's ASTROLOGICAL CALENDAR: Large 48-page wall calendar. Beautiful full-color cover and full-color paintings inside. Includes special feature articles by famous astrologers, complete introductory information on astrology, a Lunar Gardening Guide, celestial phenomena, blank horoscope chart, and monthly date pages which include aspects, Moon phases, signs and voids, planetary motion, an ephemeris, personal forecasts, lucky dates, planting and fishing dates, and more. 10 x 13 size. Set in Central time, with fold-down conversion table for other time zones worldwide.   **State year $9.95**

Llewellyn's MAGICAL ALMANAC: This beautifully illustrated almanac explores traditional earth religions and folklore while focusing on magical myths. Each month is summarized with information about the phases of the moon, festivals and rites for the month, as well as detailed magical advice. This is an indispensable guide for planning rituals, spells, and other magical events. It features writing by some of the most prominent authors in the field.   **State year $7.95**

Prices subject to change without notice.